YOUR JOURNEY TO CONSENT

*A Practical Guide to Understand,
Prevent and Heal From Sexual Violence*

Nadine Donselaar

Copyright © 2025
All Rights Reserved
No part of this book may be reproduced or transmitted in any form or by any means, electronic or mechanical, including photocopying, recording, or by any information storage and retrieval system without the written permission of the author, except where permitted by law.

For all survivors: you are not alone, there is hope.

Acknowledgment

A big thank you to you, for grabbing this book and facing such a complex, painful topic. Your courage makes the difference.

A special thank you to my parents, for welcoming back in their house after 8 years, so I could write this. To my friends, who listened to me talk about sexual violence endlessly.

And to the most special people in my life: this book wouldn't exist without you. You witnessed me breaking my own heart writing this book, offered me laughter as medicine and cheered me on with every step. I had the courage to work through this painful topic because you were there holding my hand.

Lastly, to Sara Taylor, my publishing agent: our first conversation reassured me that the world needs voices yelling about sexual violence, it empowered me to actually start writing: thank you.

Rape, one of those things we prefer not to talk about,
surrounded with guilt, shame, taboos.

Rape, we keep it hidden behind closed doors,
while the majority still believes we only have to be careful for the stranger in an allyway.

Rape, we've all heard the stories of someone who survived sexual violence.

But who actually knows the perpetrators?

Rape, a silent killer, influencing your every day.

It's not a 'women's problem, because I know men or non-binary people who are suffering too.

That one person who makes a 'stupid' sexjoke, that haunts us for weeks.

That one slap on the but in a club, that scared you to go dancing again.

Or the friends who asked you 'what were you wearing' when you finally opened up.

What if, what if we lived in a world where my body was actually just mine?

What if I could feel safe in my body again, to walk around this world?

In this book, I'll take you through a journey to understand sexual violence. This book will give you the questions, the answers are inside of yourself. See it as a guide, which includes information, journal prompts, somatic exercises, conversation starters. Personally, I had to learn these things the hard way, through trauma, rape, and years of work. I hope for this book to prevent you from suffering the way I did. Maybe even support you to create a safer world for those you love. And that way? That way we will fight this terrible global pandemic of violence, one person at a time.

We'll start by the rules, diving into law: what actually is sexual violence? What is rape? What is consent? What does Criminal Law say? And Human Rights? What do you yourself believe is morally correct?

Followed by making it more practical, and personal. What are your boundaries? How do you prevent your boundaries from being crossed? How do you make sure to respect the boundaries of others? But also: how does our society enable sexual violence to keep happening?

Lastly, we'll dive into healing from a holistic perspective. From working towards a life without the daily triggers for a survivor, to understanding the subconscious believes that justify rape. Understanding yourself, giving yourself grace, loving yourself in your mess. You might never be the person you were before, but you can be happier, wiser, more joyfull than ever.

For all of you reading this: thank you. Thank you for giving yourself, those you love, and the world, a chance on a society with one less big problem to solve. Thank you for being brave and facing a painful subject. I wish I could thank each one of you personally for doing the work with me, but for now this must do. Remember that you are loved, safe, held, supported.

Trigger warning: this book will discuss the reality of sexual violence, including examples. For survivors, or people in any way affected by this form of violence, this might be triggering. Please take those triggers seriously, comfort yourself, consult a trauma-informed professional or trusted loved one if necessary.

Reading this book, might make you realize that you have crossed boundaries of others. Seeing this, is a first step. Unfortunately, we are all capable of doing such thing. It does not make you a monster, it simply makes you human. It does give you a responsibility to do better, and to make amends with those you've hurt. It is important to acknowledge the hurt of the survivor, and put their needs above your guilt in the proces. Don't rush into big gestures or long conversations. Ask them whether they are open for a conversation on this topic before you bring it up, respect their wishes. But most of all, take your time. Finish this whole book, journal about it, talk with a loved one or professional and come from a place of balance.

Lastly, I want to note that this book is written with a focus on sexual violence between people sharing the same age. Child sexual abuse/molestation is a separate topic due to it's vulnerable nature. I would not do it justice by including it in this book, therefore this is a topic for a next book.

***

Sexual Violence

We've all heard it on the news: Rape and Sexual Harrasment. The #MeToo movement created a lot of noise a few years ago. At the moment, we even have a rise in attention for 'false accusations', sparking debates on sexual violence and consent. It's almost impossible to turn on the news and not hear something related to sexual violence: but what is it actually?

This chapter will guide you to understand what sexual violence is. This is done by giving a definition; questioning examples; understanding how it breaches Human Rights and some more of the International Law framework. I invite you to take your time this chapter to truly onderstand your own values and morals. This chapter is meant to think of why sexual violence is wrong, instead of whether it should be criminalized.

According to the World Health Organisation (WHO):

Sexual violence is "any sexual act, attempt to obtain a sexual act, or other act directed against a person's sexuality using coercion, by any person regardless of their relationship to the victim, in any setting. It includes rape, defined as the physically forced or otherwise coerced penetration of the vulva or anus with a penis, other body part or object, attempted rape, unwanted sexual touching and other non-contact forms."[1]

---

[1] World Health Organization. (2021, March 9). *Violence against women.* [Fact sheet]. https://www.who.int/news-room/fact-sheets/detail/violence-against-women.

Recent studies of 2024 showed that one in three women a romantic relationship.[2] To make this clear: if you put three women close you you - for example your grandma, mother and neighbour- together, one of them has experienced sexual violence.

Let's take a moment to see what your understanding of sexual violence is!... Put a timer on 5 minutes, grab a pen and complete the following sentence without overthinking:

Sexual violence is...

According to the WHO, Sexual Violence is one of these acts:

1. Any sexual act using coercion
2. Attempt to obtain a sexual act using coercion
3. Any other act against a person's sexualty using coercion

These three acts are not defined by the personal relationship between perpetrator and victim, nor by the setting where it happens. They specifically state the examples of rape and an attempt to rape, unwanted touching and non-contact forms.

---

[2] World Health Organization. (2021). Strengthening health systems to respond to women subjected to intimate partner violence or sexual violence: A manual for health managers (No. WHO/SRH/21.6). https://www.who.int/publications/i/item/9789240022256

The interpretation of some of these terms are difficult. What is a sexual act? When is something coercion? It's important to know that there are endless explanations for these terms. Each country has their own explanation in Criminal Law, different Human Rights Treaties have different terms. Therefore, we will explore what your perception is when you think of these problems, instead of parroting other people's thought process.

Let's make it practical! I will give an example for you for each specifically stated acts. Please note that this is not an exhaustive list. I will use Person A and Person B in these examples to keep gender out of the equation. After each example, there is some space for you to write down why this would be sexual violence in your eyes. Try to refrain from discussing criminal law or 'blame', and stay on the topic why it is sexual violence.

1. *Person A sees person B walking in a park. They follow Person B to a silent spot, pin them against a wall and starts Tongue-down-the-throat kissing Person A.*

2. *Person A sees person B in a bar, finds them attractive and buys them a drink. After some flirting back and forth, Person A realizes that they don't want to engage in a*

sexual act. Person B instigates sex multiple times, even after avoiding and a no. Person A is a little drunk, and cannot drive back home. Therefore, they accept the invitation of Person B to sleep over, while stating that they do not want to engage in any sexual act. When at home, Person B instigates sexual acts again, and Person A eventually gives in to have sex.

3. *Person A is engaged to Person B. They have a misaligned libido, and after another rejection person B breaks out in tears and says: 'You don't desire me at all! I feel so hurt, if you keep rejecting me I will break off our engagement...' Next time person B instigates sex, person A says yes without actually desiring sex.*

4. *Person A works a the company of person B. Person B often makes comments on their appearance, winks at them or makes sexual comments during workmeetings. Person A feels uncomfortable, but not in the position to stop it due to the power dynamic. Person C, a colleague, says that it is best to just laugh it off, "we should keep the workfloor fun right?!"*

5. Person A goes out for a run with her headphones on. While running in the streets of a busy city, they pass person B. Person B, a complete stranger, grabs person A's ass while they pass. Person A turns around angrily, while Person B shouts laughingly: 'great ass!'

6. Person A is in a relationship with person B, and shared some intimate pictures with them. They send them on the 'watch once' function, and is not aware that Person B screenshots the pictures and keeps them on a folder in their phone.

Let's talk about some common misconceptions about sexual violence. It's not always the scary person in an alleyway. Actually, more often it will be the person who tells you they love you the next day when they leave your house. Or your colleague who made you laugh a week before. The person that hurts you can be the person who loves you. Often, it is someone who has a relationship to you.

Sexual violence is not a 'poor people problem', nor is it just 'weak woman' who fall victim to 'bad men', there is even no racism in this exact problem. Sexual violence, is an ALL of us problem.

You might have been a perpetrator to someone else, or complicit to a situation where someone was violated. Because the 'boys will be boys' comment, when your girlfriend shared that a stranger touched her but in a club? It keeps a world intact where we condone sexual violence.

Sexual violence is a silent killer, one we look away from and act surprised when someone collapses. We might even judge a survivor who drinks a lot, uses substances and sleeps around. Or laugh at someone who shares he has a porn addiction, and says it's impossible to contain yourself if a woman is just pretty enough. Ofcourse these examples are a generalized, but, might they be alive in all of us? Are they stemming from the same problem?

So, before we dive into what's right and wrong, it's good to have a clear vision on what Sexual Violence specifically is. Read back the definition of Sexual Violence by the WHO. Afterwards: grab a pen and paper, write in the middle of the paper 'Sexual Violence' and make a wordmap with what behavior, comments and acts fall under the term.

To conclude what sexual violence is, I want to bring specific forms to your attention. This is a non-exhaustive list:

Corrective rape, which is rape of a victim in order to influence one's sexuality or gender identity.

Gang rape, where multiple perpetrators violate one survivor simultaneously.

Sexual slavery in the forms of forced marriage and confinement.

Marital rape, which takes place in intimate relationships.

Forced pregnancy or sterilization.

Genital mutilation, which is the practice of cutting the female genitals.

Force of masturbation, either done to the victim or a victim having to statisfy the perpetrator.

Forced nudity, where a victim is prohibited of wearing clothes.

Sexual Harassment, where someone kisses, touches or grabs another person unwanted.

Sexual exploitation, where a person does not only get violated, but someone else also benefits from these violations. You can see this in extreme forms as sex trafficking, but also in smaller ways as demanding sex in order for someone to get a promotion.

Sexual torture, where weapons are used on the genitals as a form of punishment.

Doxing, which is the public release of private sexual details about another person.

Forced pornography, either filming a sexual act, someone's naked body or forcing someone into the porn industry.

Generated deepfake porn used to blackmail someone.

Revenge porn, where one shares pictures without consent.

Taking pictures of someones intimate parts, without consent.

Pressuring someone into sex in exchange for a favor or using blackmail.

Sextortion, which is demanding sex in exchange for basic needs.

Sexual comments in the workplace.

Hot or not lists.

Sending unwanted nudes, sexual comments, porn.

Catcalling or making specific gestures to a stranger in the street, making sexual noises.

Threathening to sexually harass or violate another person.

Unwanted sexual comments about your body, sexuality, personality.

Sexist comments, degrading a specific gender.

Take a moment to understand what sexual violence is in your opinion. If it feels safe, and you are in a good mental place, imagine how you would feel experiencing any of this list. Reflect on whether you have been an—intentional or unintentional—perpetrator. Think about the impact these things can have on your life, and the fact that so many people on this planet experience this.

This way, you make it alive in your mind before debating why it is morally correct.

—

Next, let's find out why you believe sexual violence is wrong. To investigate your morals and values around this topic with an open mind. We will follow examples from Human Rights Treaties and Conventions.

However, this book is based on real life, not the utopia that exists written on paper. There is a big gap between the

Human Rights system and our lived experiences. Even as someone who studied Law at University for six years and has two Master Degrees - I'm sharing this for you to understand that I do actually have an understanding of the system- I see how reality is a different story. Let alone the fact that those who wrote these treaties are not representative for every human alive on this earth, but that's a story for another book!

Yet, it is still useful to use International Law as a starting point. These documents showcase what most country leaders agreed upon as morals, which we can use to create your own stance. We will look at the Universal Declaration of Human Rights. This was the first outline of the basic principles of Human Rights many countries agreed on in 1948. A declaration is a document stating certain rights, and by signing it a country is obliged to follow these guidelines in their national legal system. A country promises to respect the agreed upon statements, to protect individuals and groups from treatment that is misaligned with these agreed statements. Lastly, Countries accept the responsibility to take action to ensure that everyone get's to enjoy the agreed upon rights.

Human Rights, or Universal Rights, are inherent to being human. As a society, we decided to write them down in agreements, but it's important to understand that they are birthrights. It's a combination of rights and freedoms that belong to every human who exists on earth. They contain the basic principles, which are broader than the outlined documents that create our international legal system. Human Rights documents are simply the values, ethics we agree upon. Human Rights in itself are the 'basic principles' for life on this planet.

In the current globally accepted documents, the present religious and cultural values are present. The documents therefore are interwoven with the globally accepted worldview of the moment they were written. When working through this chaper, I want to invite you to reflect on the current modern time, and your specific environment. This might include your religion, your culture, your spiritual believes or lack thereof. Defining what is right or wrong is a deeply personl journey. Which is no surprise, if we remember that in the time of the ancient Greeks, Philosophers like Plato stated that politics and Spirituality were interconnected.[3]

It is important to remember that Sexual Violence is a global fight, one we hopefully one day all agree on and act accordingly. Personally, I believe that we comply with law more if we actually believe in it. If it is a representation of our moral ideas. With a topic as Sexual Violence, there is a big gap between reality and the legal realm. Rape is a crime, but it happens every other minute. Human Rights documents cover equality, but there is the desire to specify gender equality in new documents since reality shows dissonance between the legal system and lived experience of many women.

My invitation for this first chapter is therefore to form your own view on why sexual violence is immoral and a violation of Human Rights. Connect the information you are reading to your lived experience, make practical examples for yourself. The point is getting clear on what is morally okay for you and how to behave accordingly in the future. It might bring up some of your past mistakes, or the mistreatment you

---

[3] Lloyd P. Gerson, "Plato's Moral Realism," in *[Book Title]* (Cambridge: Cambridge University Press, 2023), 190-222, https://doi.org/10.1017/9781009329934.007.

received by others. Be gentle with yourself, find support from loved ones or professionals if these reflections are overwhelming or bring you in a dark place. If you want to make amends with someone you hurted, please be respectful of their process. Always ask whether it is okay to bring this topic up, and respect their wishes in the way a conversation is held or possible lack of conversation.

The first article of the Universal Declaration of Human Rights states:

"All human beings are born free and equal in dignity and rights. They are endowed with reason and conscience and should act towards one another in a spirit of brotherhood."[4]

Followed by the second article which states:

"Everyone is entitled to all the rights and freedoms set forth in this Declaration, without distinction of any kind, such as race, colour, sex, language, religion, political or other opinion, national or social origin, property, birth or other status. Furthermore, no distinction shall be made on

---

[4] United Nations General Assembly. (1948). *Universal Declaration of Human Rights*, Article 1. https://www.un.org/en/about-us/universal-declaration-of-human-rights

the basis of the political, jurisdictional or international status of the country or territory to which a person belongs, whether it be independent, trust, non-self-governing or under any other limitation of sovereignty." [5]

And the third article that states:

"Everyone has the right to life, liberty and security of person" [6]

Amnesty (one of the leading Human Rights Organizations) made a simplified version:

Article 1: All human beings are born free and equal.

Article 2: Everyone is equal regardless of race, colour, sex, language, religion, politics, or where they were born.

Article 3: Everyone has the right to life (and to live in freedom and safety). [7]

Let's connect these statements with a real life situation. Grab a pen and paper, and write everything that comes up with the following journalprompt: If you tell your partner no,

---

[5] UN General Assembly (1948), Art. 2.

[6] UN General Assembly (1948), Art. 3.

[7] Amnesty International. (n.d.). *Universal Declaration of Human Rights.* https://www.amnesty.org/en/what-we-do/universal-declaration-of-human-rights/

and they insist on having sex, do they behave according to these articles?

Based on the fact you picked up this book, you probably thought that this question has an easy answer: 'No is a complete sentence'; 'My body is mine'; 'Someone who respects you, should step back', 'My desire is not someone else's responsibility' might be some of the thoughts that crossed your mind.

But in reality, we should acknowledge that there are a lot of different outcomes to a situation like this. Not that no is not a full sentence, but because life is not a perfect book example. Imagine this:

You have been together for a long time, and your libido does not match. When someone rejects you for the 5th time in a row, you might think: "I know you will have fun once we start, let me just try again."

You meet someone in the bar, and they try to kiss you, all flirty, you tell them no. You want to make them work a little harder for that kiss. You want them to insist, because it might make you feel more desired.

Your Journey to Consent

You grew up in a society, or religion, where one believed that the male opinion is worth more than a women's. Without being aware of it, you expect a women to comply with a males desire.

Would these occasions change your answer to the question? Does this mean you do not agree with the Human Rights?

Sexual violence is not always done with bad intend. Sometimes, people who would say that a no is a no, act differently because of subconscious believes. Therefore, I ask of you to be completely honest with yourself in this process of finding your moral opinion on this matter. Take into consideration that this might be confronting, but the pain of keeping the current situation intact is worse than the discomfort of changing it.

To circle back to the globally accepted norms, we'll get into both articles with the exercise in the back of our mind.

"All human beings are born free and equal in dignity and rights"

This gives everyone the inherent right to freedom and equality. Both terms are used very frequently, and in many different circumstances. But what do they actually mean? What is freedom? What is equality?

Freedom is often described as living in full autonomy. This means that you get to decide how you live your life. The big boundary to freedom is when it crossess someone else's rights and way of living. Here is the grey zone: Where does your freedom end and someone else's start? Which prevails?

In International Law, the system of law Human Rights falls under, they look at principles in a way of positive (to act) and negative (to obstain) from the perspective of the government. This means that for us civilians, freedom exists in the way to live your life without interference. On the other side, we have a right to receive support in order to live in Freedom.

An important form of freedom is physical freedom, not being limited in where you live and what you do. But also the freedom of opinion: to believe what is right to you and to express this to others, ofcourse with limitations.

Freedom in regards to sexual violence means being able to say yes or no according to what feels right to you. It means that your body belongs to you, and you decide what to do with it. Simply said: if you want to engage in sexual acts with another person, you can. If you do not want to engage in sexual acts with another person, you don't have to. This comes with the obligation for others to respect your personal autonomy over your body, and the obligation for the government to prevent sexual violence from happening.

Equality can be seen as the right to be treated as anyone else in the same situation. Please notice the nuance: 'in the same situation'. In todays world, this will not always mean that everyone get's treated the exact same. We live in a world where unfortunately there are differences in opportunities for different groups of people. This can lead to having different solutions in different situations, for equal treatment.

Being equal in dignity and rights means having the same autonomy over your life no matter your cultural, geographical, sexual background. It shows that Human Rights are exactly the same for everyone. For the legal system, it comes with the obligation to use the law in a way that doesn't discriminate. For the government it comes with the obligation to ensure that the system works fair for all, ensuring equal chances and opportunities.

If one extends this to sexual violence, this simply means that every person has equal opportunity to say yes or no to any sexual act. No matter ones gender, sexuality, race or religion: everyones sexual freedom is worth the same. Therefore, you cannot force someone into complying with your desires, since their desires are equally as important. A yes never outweighs a no, even if you have all the reason in the world to believe that your yes is grounded in reason. If the other person is equal to you, you cannot do anything than agree to disagree and part ways.

The principles of equality and freedom are intertwined. How can you be free, if another person is not? Meaning, how can you be free in your choice to have sex, but force another person to engage in your desires? If both parties are free to choose what they do with their bodies, is it fair to have an expectation of their choice? Is it reasonable to not have expectations? How do you behave in sexual situations, if you truly believe all parties deserve equal space for expression? How can you ensure the freedom of expression for both parties in an equal way? If this even possible?

There is no equality, if you don't have freedom. How can both parties be equal, if one does not have the opportunity to speak freely? How can you believe that both are equal, if you don't leave the other person the freedom to choose what they do with their body? Is there equality, if there are unspoken rules to comply with in a sexual setting? For example: a man is dominant and a woman complies with his desires? Or the social idea that rejecting someone is 'bad'? Or the idea that it is 'cool' to have lots of sex; or the oposite: that it is 'gross' and takes away from your worth?

Take a moment to sink into your body and the present moment. By going for a walk, doing a childspose for 10 minutes, doing some box-breathing (6 seconds in - hold 6 seconds - 6 seconds out- hold 6 seconds, always through the nose all the way into the belly).

After this, answer the following three journal prompts, take 5 minutes for each one:

- *How does sexual violence interfere with the right to freedom?*
- *How does sexual violence interfere with the equality in dignity and rights?*
- *In what way are these two answers connected with each other?*

The second part of this article in the Universal Declaration of Human Rights goes into the interaction between two people: *"They are endowed with reason and conscience and should act towards one another in a spirit of brotherhood."*

Human Rights are based in reason and logic, but also in consciousness and our heart. This shows the double foundation of our rights in values and logic. What is a logical reason for everyone to have the same rights and dignity? Which philosophical ideas can you come up with and resonate with you? It also shows how we should act in relationship to others: in a way that aligns with reason and moral believes.

Sex is oftentimes seen as an 'emotional' or 'desire' matter, but still we have to behave with reason and conscience. This means that we cannot state that our desire for another person blinded us for their no. This also shows that even in the heat of the moment we have to treat people with respect, keeping our morals and values in the back of our mind.

To conclude this, when making a decision on whether or not to have sex, one should use their rational mind, and ethical views. Maybe it can be good to take a moment with yourself to think on this. What conditions do you rationally find important to decide to have sex with someone? Which values do you have when it comes to sex? What feels unethical for you in the bedroom? These are big questions, but necessary to answer. Keep in mind that the answers don't have to be vast, your opinions can change overtime.

Your Journey to Consent

In line with this, we have the birthright to be treated with respect of our freedom and equality in rights and dignity. Which gives us full autonomy over our body, and everyone who would engage in sexual acts with us, should treat us with respect, and in a way where they perceive us as equal.

We are the only person who decides what happens to our body. We are allowed to take up space, demand respect as long as it is whitin reason. We have the obligation to make our mind up on the values we want to live by, and treat others the way we want to be treated. This comes with repaying the favor, and treating everyone the way you wish to be treated.

Lastly, in an interaction between two people, you should act in the spirit of brotherhood. Historically, this brings us back to the idea that everyone is part of the same family. It is supposed to call in unity for all, and a feeling of connection where everyone treats each other from a place of love. Another phrasing is to act in solidarity with each other. Simpler said: we all have to support each other and look out for each other.

However, there is a current debate whether the word brotherhood is not outdated. It showcases the spirit of time in which the agreement was created.[8] In this time, there was a priority for men over women in society. The gendered norms are crosswise opposite to the idea of equality. This is a subject we'll further discuss when we get to 'rape-culture'.

If we act in solidarity and unity with each other, we wouldn't want to make sexist comments, sexually harass or rape another person. This idea goes beyond freedom and equality. This comes from wanting to make the other person feel good, to treat them like family. A perpetrator who looks at the victim from a place of love, would most likely behave in a different manner. In a way, solidarity can even be seen as uplifting each other. We wouldn't want to bring down a person we love, how can we then take away their freedom, or treat them as if they are less than ourselves.

Look back at the list you made in one of the previous exercise stating what behaviors are sexual violence in your perception. For each of them, come up with why they go against acting based on reason and values, or solidarity.

---

[8] Ward, S. (2025, February 2). *Article 1 UDHR: Brotherhood in human rights law*. Ward Blawg. https://wardblawg.com/2025/02/02/article-1-udhr-brotherhood-human-rights-law/

Having a clear vision on what sexual violence is, and why it is inherently wrong, makes it easier to understand why this problem is asking for our attention. By making sure you understand your own opinion, it's easier to be actively involved in discussions on the topic.

Sexual violence is one of the most intimate and impactful violations of our human rights possible. Whether it is being raped, having a naked picture shared, being touched, receiving condoning comments after speaking up or anything in between: someone breaches your right to freedom and equality in this moment. It can be in a smal way, or more elaborate; it can affect you for a day or a lifetime. This does not change that these acts are inherently wrong.

And indirectly, it violates the social contract we as a society have to treat each other with respect. The people around the survivor get affected by the violation as well: whether it is by the aftermath, the fear that it installs, or second-hand rage. Sexual violation towards one person, impacts the understanding of freedom and equality for all.

All of us, as part of society, have the responsibility to treat others with respect. This includes ensuring not to violate someone else's bodily autonomy. The government has the responsibility to ensure that we get treated in this way. Criminal law is a way to punish this behavior after it has happened. Which gives off the message to others not to do this, and might give a feeling of retaliation for the victim. However, the responsibility to protect also enholds prevention, education, support for survivors and challenge any norm that enables sexual violence.

—

As concluded in the previous paragraph, sexual violence breaches the principle of equality. Article 2 of the UDHR explains this further in the following way: *"Everyone is entitled to all the rights and freedoms set forth in this Declaration, without distinction of any kind, such as race, colour, sex, language, religion, political or other opinion, national or social origin, property, birth or other status."*[9]

Gender-based violence is a big part of sexual violence, but before we dive into this, I do want to pinpoint that there is more we have to fight than sexual violence against women. Men experience sexual violence. Young boys get molested. In the grey area, which we will get into later in this book, men

---

[9] UN General Assembly (1948), Art. 2.

fall victim to unconsensual sex just like women. In this book, the terms survivor/victim and perpetrator are not bound to gender.

However, we cannot ignore the incredibly high numbers for women: 1 in 3 women experience either intimate partner violence or rape by the hands of an unknown perpetrator.[10] This means that if you ask your mother, grandmother and aunt, most likely one of them has experienced this violence. Therefore, we will get into women's rights and discrimination based on gender.

Another perspective is the concept of intersectionality. Where in the following paragraphs I will focus on discrimination against women, a white, cis-gendered, able-bodied woman deals with discrimination based on gender. Racism, colonialism, social status, sexual preference, financial position, skintone, religion can make a huge difference and in many instances work against someone.

We live in a system which unfortunately is not based on equal opportunities for everyone. Different forms of discrimination or oppression overlap in real life. This means

---

[10] See footnote 1.

that the problems someone experiences due to racism and gender influence and worsen each other. For example: a black, disabled woman deals with discrimination in three different ways. In real life, these are not three separate problems, they show up as one.

Some other examples are: the fetishization of specific races, leading to more sexual violence and hatecrimes against women of a specific background. Lingering colonial ideals, leading to a rise in sexual violence due to the believe that they are worth less. The bigger risk for women who are disabled to be targetted. Survivors who are silenced to protect the reputation of a religious community, or bribed with money to keep quite.

Unfortunately, solving one problem will not solve another. For this book, I will focus on gendered discrimination. However, I do want to recommend you to dive into other forms of discrimination along the way. Freedom and Equality go hand in hand, your path to freedom get's influenced by how equally free everyone else on the world is. The privilege of not experiencing certain types of discrimination, comes with the responsibility of understanding and actively fighting it.

Especially with the current state of the world, I want to offer the perspective that staying silent oftentimes means choosing the side of the perpetrator. By complying with wrongful behavior, for whichever reason, we create a situation that enables this behavior to continue. Being able to stay silent and 'focussing on happiness' is a privilege. Keep in mind what you would want if you were in the other position. And a last note: if you want to speak up for others, focus on amplifying their voices instead of sharing your opinion. A woman knows what she needs, and as a man you can share her voice towards the world. People need support, not saving.

With the following quote, I want to break the stigma that only 'weak', 'helpless', or 'financial dependent' women fall victim to sexual violence: *"Violence against women is perhaps the most shameful human rights violation, and it is perhaps the most pervasive. It knows no boundaries of geography, culture or wealth. As long as it continues, we cannot claim to be making real progress towards equality, development and peace"* - Kofi Annan. This quote is from 1999, and in today's world we are still battling the same problem.

It brings me to share that there is sexual violence in every country, in every religion, in every culture and no matter someone's financial situation. We do have to acknowledge that there are different forms of sexual violence more prevalent in different social groups. However, sexual violence is not something we can pretend doesn't happen in our own bubble.

Before we will discuss the role discrimination based on gender has, it's good to form your own opinion. Spend some time to reflect on your perspective of sexual violence by answering the following journalprompts: Is sexual violence in a personal attack or a gendered-based attack? How does gendered discrimination influence sexual violence? Which role does this play in finding a solution to the problem?

—

Sexual violence disproportionately affects women and girls more. Globally, the number of instances where a woman is the survivor in a reported sexual violence situation is substantionally higher. The convention on the Elimination of All Forms of Discrimination agains Women (CEDAW), adopted by the UN general Assembly is the leading global agreements in women's rights. This document is a broad anti-discrimination agreement and focuses on the equal position of women. The agreement does not directly mention violence against women, the prohibition for it can be interpreted in the original text and there are multiple additional documents written by the Committeee which explain the global moral on sexual violence.[11]

These documents give States the legal obligation to create a legal framework to create a legal framework which criminalizes sexual violence and fights the underlying problem, while giving the necessary attention to age and gender.[12] If a State signs CEDAW, it's in the line of expectation that they agree with the commentary on sexual violence as well; however it is not given. Unfortunately, we also deal with the gap in legal and life reality. Many countries have signed CEDAW, however: women still experience discrimination in all forms. Make an effort to assay the values written in this paragraph to the unfolding reality you live. How do you see differences in treatment based on gender in your day-to-day life?

---

[11] Committee on the Elimination of Discrimination Against Women. (1992). *General recommendation No. 19: Violence against women* (para. 6). United Nations. https://www.refworld.org/docid/52d920c54.html

[12] Committee on the Elimination of Discrimination Against Women. (2017). *General recommendation No. 35 on gender-based violence against women, updating general recommendation No. 19*. United Nations. https://documents-dds-ny.un.org/doc/UNDOC/GEN/N17/231/54/PDF/N1723154.pdf?OpenElement

Regionally, there are three additional agreements: one in the Americana's; one in Africa and one in Europe. These give additional obligations and nuances to the human rights situation. In Latin-America, there is the Belém do Pará convention, which specifically states that sexual violence is a human rights violation. It additionally states that women have the right to live free from stereotypes and inferiority, something that touches the core of sexual violence: rape-culture.[13] This convention gives the additional obligation to take into consideration the role of intersectionality.[14]

In Africa there is the extra protocol to the African Charter on Human and People's Rights regarding special protecBon for women (Maputo Protocol). In this protocol there is a specific obligation to protect against violence, including harmful practices.[15] It additionally states that there should be

---

[13] Organization of American States. (1994). *Inter-American Convention on the Prevention, Punishment and Eradication of Violence against Women* ("Convention of Belém do Pará"), Article 3 &
6. https://www.oas.org/juridico/english/treaties/a-61.html

[14] OAS (1994), Art. 9.

[15] African Union. (2003). *Protocol to the African Charter on Human and Peoples' Rights on the Rights of Women in Africa* ("Maputo Protocol"), preamble, jo. African Charter art.

legal, institutional and other measures, which broadens the spectrum to all kinds of policies to prevent sexual violence.[16]

In Europe there is the Istanbul Convention which is specifically for prevention and combatting of violence against women. It acknowledges the historical unequal roles of man and women and it's impact on sexual violence.[17] It includes that the created framework has attention for a holistic response for survivors, and States have the obligation to make enough financial resources to do so.[18] It also includes that the police interrogation has to proceed in a way that takes the rights of a survivor into consideration.[19]

This short overview showcases how the rights of women is more explecitly described in newer international agreements. It shows how there is more importance for the position of women in sexual violence. Unfortunately, these

---

18(3). https://au.int/en/treaties/protocol-african-charter-human-and-peoples-rights-rights-women-africa

[16] AU (2003), Art. II(b) jo. Art. I(g).

[17] Council of Europe. (2011). Convention on preventing and combating violence against women and domestic violence ("Istanbul Convention"), preamble. https://rm.coe.int/168008482e

[18] Council of Europe (2011), Art. 7(1) & 8.

[19] Council of Europe (2011), Art. 49 jo. 50.

legal agreements have not sufficiently affected the real life situation.

Activists are advocating for a new, global, human rights framework which protects women against violence: an optional protocol called Every Woman Treaty.[20] This would strengthen the legal position of women globally, and protect activists who are fighting for women's rights.[21] This specific treaty focuses on having the right to life a live without violence. There is specific focus for the access to justice and the possibility to speak up. An important detail is that this is made by female voices, since the team who created this proposal legal framework is are mostly female activists and scholars. This document focuses on measurements that require to raise awareness, condemn violence, protect women, and improve cooperation between different institutions and women. These norms, and domestic measurements, must be made with women in the lead.

---

[20] EveryWoman Treaty. (n.d.). Optional protocol to accelerate elimination of gender-based violence. https://everywoman.org/optional-protocol/#publication

[21] Aeberhard-Hodges, J., Ayoubi, N., & Rivera Juaristi, F. J. (2023). Safer now: Rapid rise in violence against women and girls demands highest level of global commitment (p. 5). Every Woman Treaty.

These nuances are focused on closing the gap between reality and the legal framework. It is important to have clear guidelines for measurements. If you would be able to make a change: what would you focus on? Practical solutions or a new legal framework?

These short overviews gave a more clear and practical overview of legal requirements specific International agreements give for States. Which ones resonate with you most? What would you write in these International Agreements if you were in power?

One thing these documents show, is that unfortunately women have to be protected against sexual violence. Globally, our political leaders feel the need to fight this problem, and acknowledge that it is rooted in gender discrimination. In my opinion, you can state that these rights extend to men as well if they are victim of sexual violence. Therefore, this shows a broader scope of legal protection against sexual violence in general.

Take a moment to check-in with yourself: sit down relaxed and take a few deep breaths. When you feel present, ask yourself: how does this information make you feel? Which emotions come up and how does this feel in your body?

Afterwards, answer the following questions: Which role should women have in the route to finding a solution to this gut-wrenching problem? And which role do the other genders have?

—

Based on Article 3 of the UDHR, we al have *'the right to life, liberty and security of person'* It means that you have the right to be alive, to move around freely and to keep your body safe. This therefore also prohibits others from infringing this right, covering the prohibition of sexual violence. This gives you the right to bodily autonomy and integrity. Autonomy gives you the opportunity to decide what happens to your body, and who gets to touch your body. Integrity guarantees you the protection against an infringement to this right.

If we consider everyone to have bodily autonomy, it means that you have the right to decide what you do with your body without the influence of anyone else. There has to be consent in order to engage in sexual acts. Consent has become a popular term in todays world, and it's important to understand what consent means. Understanding consent makes it easier to shift our perception from having to harnass yourself against sexual violence to being able to prevent sexual violence by understanding consent. To have freedom of rape, means that we recognize sex without consent as rape.[22]

If we combine the right to bodily autonomy with the right to freedom and equality as discussed prior to this, we can conclude that a good legal system should ensure that everyone is completely free, and has the opportunity to decide what happens to their bodies as long as this does not infringe anyone else's rights.

For States, this would mean that they have the obligation to protect our possibility to uphold this standard. In real life situations, we have to respect others in a way that they feel free to decide who gets to touch their body at all times. It ensures us that nobody 'owns' our body except us.

Consent is actually not only a human right, it is one of the foundational principles to human rights: *'Bodily autonomy – the ability for people to make their own choices about their bodies, including on issues relating to health care, contraception and whether to have sex – is not only a human*

---

[22] Amnesty International. (2018, April 12). *EU: Sex without consent is rape.* https://www.amnesty.org/en/latest/news/2018/04/eu-sex-without-consent-is-rape/

right, but *the foundation* upon which other human rights are built.'[23]

Consent, specifically affirmative consent, can be explained as the following: *'Affirmative consent must be an active, voluntary, informed, and mutual decision to engage in sexual activity. Consent can be given through clear words or actions through which a person has indicated permission to engage in sexual activity. Affirmative Consent should be clear and enthusiastic, rather than simply the absence of a "no". Affirmative consent can be withdrawn at any time, and cannot be obtained by expressed or implied force, threats, or coercion.'*[24]

Another explanation of consent can be a yes which is: *'Enthousiastic, given freely, informed, specific, and revirsible'*

---

[23] United Nations Population Fund. (n.d.). *Five things you need to know about consent.* https://www.unfpa.org/news/five-things-you-need-know-about-consent#:~:text=Bodily%20autonomy%20%E2%80%93%20the%20ability%20for,other%20human%20rights%20are%20built

[24] Right to Equality. (n.d.). *Affirmative consent campaign.* https://righttoequality.org/campaign/affirmative-consent/

[25] In the Istanbul Convention, Europes convention protecting against violence against women and domestic violence, states that rape is the absence of freely given consent.[26]

Consent is not just a 'modern concept', it is actually rooted in human rights. Let's reflect a little more on this subject to find your perspective. Grab a pen and paper and answer the following questions: How would you describe consent in sexual settings, based on the concept of bodily autonomy? According to this explanation, which obligations do you believe that States have to protect their citizens from sexual violence? And how do you as an individual have to show up in sexual settings, based on this understanding of consent?

—

Even though this book is not about the punishment of sexual violence, I do want to inform you on criminal law. This way you can inform yourself on the situation in your country and speak up if it feels right. Hearing about these cases makes

---

[25] UN Women. (2019, November). *Consent: No blurred lines*. https://www.unwomen.org/en/news/stories/2019/11/feature-consent-no-blurred-lines

[26] Council of Europe. (2023, November 22). *Statement by Secretary-General Alain Berset* [Press release]. https://www.coe.int/en/web/istanbul-convention/-/statement-by-secretary-general-alain-berset

it more clear in what ways sexual violence shows up in the world and how severe the problem can be.

Before diving into the punishment sexual violence against one victim, I want to bring your attention to something that happens on a bigger scale. Sexual violence gets used as a weapon. Let that sink in. Sexual violence is classified as a Crime against Humanity, War Crime and Genocide at the International Criminal Court.[27] In the agreements for armed conflict, they specified that rape is prohibited.[28] Rape also falls under the scope of the Convention Against Torture, meaning that it gets used as torture.

We're not just talking about individual experiences, there have been, and are still happening, occasions where men, women and children get sexually assaulted or raped as part of a 'plan' in conflicts. Taking away someone's dignity and bodily autonomy is seen as a weapon, due to the immense impact this has on one's life.

---

[27] International Criminal Court. (1998). *Rome Statute of the International Criminal Court*, Articles 6, 7 & 8. https://www.icc-cpi.int/sites/default/files/RS-Eng.pdf

[28] International Committee of the Red Cross. (1949/1977). *Geneva Conventions of 1949 and Additional Protocols*, Common Article 3 (GC I-IV), Additional Protocol I Article 76, Additional Protocol II Article 4. https://ihl-databases.icrc.org/en/ihl-treaties

Current examples of this are seen in the Russia-Ukraine war. In the start of this conflict, many cases of rape and sexual violence where reported, leading the UN special representative of the secretary-general on sexual violence in conflict to state that Russia is using it as a military strategy in order to dehumanize the victim.[29]

Amnesty International reported that in Tigray forces use several forms of sexual violence against women and girls as a weapon of war, in an attempt to terrorize, degrade and dehumanize.[30] The United Nation reports cases of severe sexual violence, including gang-rape, of detained Palestinians in Israels prisons.[31] Unicef reports that every 30 minutes, a child in the Democratic Republic of the Congo gets raped in a

---

[29] Busol, K. (2024, March 25). *Russia is weaponising sexual violence – and Ukraine's values are being eroded in the process.* The Guardian. https://www.theguardian.com/commentisfree/2024/mar/25/russia-weaponising-sexual-violence-ukraine-values

[30] Kapp, C. (2022, November 1). *The devastating use of sexual violence as a weapon of war.* Think Global Health. https://www.thinkglobalhealth.org/article/devastating-use-sexual-violence-weapon-war

[31] Office of the High Commissioner for Human Rights. (2024, August [dd]). *Israel's escalating use of torture against Palestinians in custody is preventable* [Press release]. https://www.ohchr.org/en/press-releases/2024/08/israels-escalating-use-torture-against-palestinians-custody-preventable

very systematic way.[32] The United Nations reports that in Myanmar, sexual acts get demanded from women as a condition to have their husbands released from detainment.[33]

These are just some examples of reported ways in which sexual violence is used on a systematic scale as a weapon. This happens in smaller ways as well, whitin communities, or in specific neighborhoods.

Sexual violence also happens on a systemic, or large scale outside of armed conflict. Examples are the broad range of cases of child sexual abuse in the Roman Catholic Church[34];

---

[32] United Nations Children's Fund. (2025, April 11). *A child reported raped every half hour in eastern DRC as violence rages amid growing funding gaps* [Press release]. https://www.unicef.org/press-releases/child-reported-raped-every-half-hour-eastern-drc-violence-rages-amid-growing-funding

[33] UN Secretary-General's Report on Conflict-Related Sexual Violence: [1]United Nations. (2024). Conflict-related sexual violence: Report of the Secretary-General (S/2024/292). https://reliefweb.int/report/world/conflict-related-sexual-violence-report-secretary-general-s2024292-enarruzh

[34] ICSA Roman Catholic Church Investigation Executive Summary: [3]Independent Inquiry into Child Sexual Abuse. (2020). Roman Catholic Church investigation: Executive summary. https://www.iicsa.org.uk/reports-recommendations/publications/investigation/roman-catholic-church/executive-summary.html

the endless stories of rape and sexual violence in prison[35]; alleged systematic sexual violence against Uyghurs in China[36]; the use of sexual violence to fight the uprise 'Woman Life Freedom' in Iran[37]; an increase of human trafficking, where a significant amount of the victims get sexually exploited[38]; and lastly, there are still many cases of childbrides worldwide. Sexual violence ruins lives on a personal level, but also a societal level.

Take a moment and try to grasp the severity of this information. These are situations still hapening in todays world. Sexual violence as a weapon, as means to a goal. Sexual violence as a systematic problem in this world. Did you realize the

---

[35] Human Rights Watch. (2001). *No escape: Male rape in U.S. prisons.* https://www.hrw.org/reports/2001/prison/report1.html

[36] Human Rights Watch. (2021, April 19). *"Break their lineage, break their roots": China's crimes against humanity targeting Uyghurs and other Turkic Muslims.* https://www.hrw.org/report/2021/04/19/break-their-lineage-break-their-roots/chinas-crimes-against-humanity-targeting

[37] Amnesty International. (2023, December 12). *Iran: Security forces used rape and other sexual violence to crush 'Woman, Life, Freedom' uprising with impunity.* https://www.amnesty.org/en/latest/news/2023/12/iran-security-forces-used-rape-and-other-sexual-violence-to-crush-woman-life-freedom-uprising-with-impunity/

[38] United Nations. (2025, March 12). Human Rights Council: Significant increase in child victims of trafficking [News story]. https://news.un.org/en/story/2025/03/1161061

problem was this big? Did you know this is such a huge scaled problem, in many places of the world?

Grab a pen and paper and reflect how this information makes you feel. What does it show you of the state of the world? What does it tell you on how the world sees sex? How severe does this problem feel?

Rape and sexual violence against an individual is prohibited in most countries, and punishable under criminal law. The way these laws are written makes a huge difference in interpretation. It can be a good idea therefore, to read the articles making sexual violence illegal in your country before continueing to read this book. This will give you a clear idea on the common stance in your situation with regards to this pervasive violation of autonomy.

There are different ways sexual offences are criminalized. In some countries the focus is on penetration, in other countries there is a varied list of offences, which is regardless of penetration. In some countries it is necessary to proof that the sexual acts was a result of 'use of force'. In other places it focuses on consensual sex.

In some countries rape whitin a marriage is illegal since less than a 100 years, since Poland was the first country to make this illegal in 1932. Most countries who specifically illegalized this, were years later in the second wave of feminism around the 1970's.[39] In other countries rape whitin marriage is legal or grounds for reduced sentences. In some countries settlement outside of court is still possible, in some countries rape becomes legal if the survivor and perpetrator marry each other. Some laws are gender neutral, where other laws ignore male or LGBTQ+ groups. New forms of sexual violence, for example online, are not always criminalized yet. In some countries they ban non-consensual porn, but in many places there is no specific law for these modern-day problems.

The differences in law are too broad to specifically comment on them. However, a global problem is the failure to prosecute predators. Less than 40 percent seek any form of support, and less than 10 percent of those seeking help actually make it to the police.[40] When women go to the police, it is not given that they are taken seriously, or have enough proof to make it a prosecutable case.

Simultaneously, there is a movement now that feels like the new laws, which are consent-based, are a threath to men.

---

[39] LHSS Collective. (n.d.). *Marital rape: A crime undefined.* https://lhsscollective.in/marital-rape-a-crime-undefined/

[40] United Nations Statistics Division. (2015). *The World's Women 2015: Violence against women* (Chapter 6). https://unstats.un.org/unsd/gender/downloads/WorldsWomen2015_chapter6_t.pdf

That the numbers of 'fake' accusations get higher since victims are seeking revenge, or money. Where I do acknowledge that this might be true in some cases, I feel that this is taking the attention away from the reel problem: people get sexualy violated on a very regular basis. This new narrative is a form of rape-culture, a topic we will discuss later.

Even in countries where there are laws prohibiting and punishing sexual violence, the problem remains the same. I would recommend you to seek some information on the discussions in the country where you currently live: if you experience sexual violence, how can you report? What are the prerequisitives for getting someone convicted? This is information that is good to have clear for yourself or those around you when you experience sexual violence. It also gives you some bedding to protest if, you feel that the criminal system in your country does not comply with human rights or is insufficient. Knowledge is power.

For those who have experienced sexual violence, but never made it to court or decided not to report it. Your experience is valid, the pain you have experienced does not need to be validated by the justice system. You are allowed to decide what is right to you, also if that means never reporting your perpetrator.

—

Your Journey to Consent

What is right, what is wrong

So many perceptions, yet one clear rule

You have the freedom to decide what sexual acts you want to do,

And so does everyone else with you.

Why? You might ask,

That's up to you to answer.

Where are the boundaries? What is the grey zone?

Up for discussion in every nation, in every culture.

Criminal law, Human Rights, So much to uncover,

Yet it all comes together to something bigger.

Treat eachother from a place of love and respect,

Don't let your desire override someone else's safety.

***

How do you prevent sexual violence?

How do we stop this pandemic of sexual violence? A problem that is so taboo, embedded in society, surrounded by questionmarks. Even if a country has signed a Human Rights Treaty fighting sexual violence, even if it is illegal according to criminal law: how do you enforce this on citizens? While you were reading this sentence, someone else has been harrassed or raped, causing their whole life to change by the hands of another person.

As someone who studied law, I would love for the world to decide on signing a new treaty like the Every Woman Now Treaty.[41] A globally accepted legal framework, which would bring clarity in what is right, and what is not. Clarity in this way would give survivors a fighting chance to justice. As a Reiki Master and Kundalini Yoga Teacher, I wish for everyone to find their way of creating internal balance. This way, people are less likely to perpetrate others, and hopefully refind peace after surviving a nightmare. As a young woman, I'm angry. How can we as a society evolve so much, create the most intricate technology, yet still ruin each other's life in such a stupid way?

---

[41] Every Woman Treaty. (n.d.). *Homepage.* https://everywoman.org/

Unfortunately, only a new legal treaty wouldn't be the solution. The legal situation is often times far away from reality, where even if it is clearly illegal: it happens. Life is more than the rules and policies we create. It's common knowledge that most cases never make it to the police, so where strenghtening criminal laws is useful, it is not sufficient. We need to focus on prevention. Prevention in my opinion starts smal, in yourself. Which is exactly what you are doing by diving into this topic.

Thank you, for taking the time to understand this topic. Thank you, for opening your eyes to this problem. Thank you, for making this world a better place. In this chapter, we will start by finding ways to harnass yourself against sexual violence, from there we will move to how to find ways in relationships and afterwards we will go into how to prevent sexual violence in general and ways to dismantle 'rape-culture'.

Please understand, that experiencing sexual violence is not your fault. It's not wrong if you freeze and do have the capacity to say a clear no. It's not your fault if you found yourself in a situation that is dangerous. Ofcourse, there are nuances and we always have a responsibility for ourselves, but that does not make us the one to carry the guilt.

On top of that, being respected in our boundaries has not only to do with ourselves. You can be 'strong and confident', and still get sexualy violated. The questions: 'what were you wearing'; 'were you intoxicated?'; 'Did you say no?' Are unfair, not valid, and retraumatizing. To give it to you straight: it's a form of sexual violence.

The reason this chapter still starts with yourself, is because we are unfortunately unable to change anything or anyone besides ourselves. We can try to bring change into society, but for this we have to be centered and secure in ourelves. In the end, it's always the other person themselves deciding to reflect, and hopefully change, based on a conversation. All we can do is be clear in our boundaries and what we allow to exist in our life.

Especially in sexual violence, it is important to fully comprehend why you find specific values and norms important. It is very common to state you are against sexual violence, but subconsciously or indirectly still add to the problem. For example by pushing your romantic partner to have sex: "but I know you will enjoy it and we haven't had sex in forever!". Or by not taking someone who opens up to you seriously: "boys will be boys, it's part of life to get touched on the but!". If we want this problem to dissolve, we need everyone fully on board.

The very first step in preventing sexual violence is getting to know yourself. What do you like? What are your desires? What do you believe to be okay or not okay? What are your boundaries? The answers to those questions are not static, they keep evolving and change as you grow older. Sexual boundaries are a lifelong exploration of yourself. And, these are things we can't just answer with the mind. We have to feel it in our body, learn to listen to our body, build a relationship with our body in order to do so.

So, before we start overthinking: let's hear the body talk!

Start by putting the book, your phone and anything that can distract you away. Find yourself a spoth that is quiet, and where you will not be disturbed for a little while. Prepare some nice, relaxing music, maybe even some candles and incense. Start by shaking the body for 5-10 minutes. Yes I know it sounds weird, but it helps you to get all the stress out. Shake the legs, the arms, the whole body, jump around, breath in and out heavily, sigh, scream, whatever makes you feel relaxed and present in this moment.

Afterwards, find yourself a comfortable position, maybe you want to sit in childspose for a bit, do a butterfly position, sit straight up or lay down back on your neck. Take deep breaths through the nose, into the belly.

First think of sex, where do you feel this in the body? What sensations, emotions come up? Slowly allow your hands to wander around your body: what feels nice, what does not feel nice? Allow yourself to get lost in the moment, and figure out which nice and less nice things come up.

Keep in mind that this exercise can have different effects: some might feel it's exciting, other may relive negative experiences. It's good to realize all times that you are doing this for yourself, you do not have to continue if it doesn't feel good. And, you can redo this exercise as often as you want: not everything needs to be discovered at the same time! You have a whole lifetime to figure out what sex is to you.

Having a relationship with your own body first, helps to listen to the body when you are in a connection with someone else. Sex is something we should feel, not something we perform. Nowadays, we often base our ideas on porn, movies, stories. In this book, we're looking for real pleasure from the bottom of your toes, not the acted, wattered down or forced version of it. It's not strange to pleasure yourself, even if you have a relationship. It can actually help you to understand your 'full body yes' better, the key for consensual sex!

Have you taken the time to look into different forms of sex, and what sounds interesting to you and what not? It's time to reclaim authority in your sexlife. Sex and intimacy consists of a whole buffet of possibilities. Penetration, the classic cis-gendered;straight sex is one dish, but there is more to discover!

Google different types of sex: Vanilla sex, Kinks, BDSM, Non-penetrative variations. You can read about it in magazines, in some fiction books, watch ethical (!) porn. Another possibility is to google different sexual fantasies and see how they make you feel, does it sound attractive to you? You can find the different erogenous zones and touch them, to see how these feel for you. Do your research, don't forget to have fun with it! Keep in mind that we are creating a starting point here, just an idea of what you would be interested in at this moment. Sexual preferences can develop or disappear over time.

Sexual violence doesn't only show up in very apparant ways. It can be in the details of a moment, that throws you off.

A pressure in between the lines, the specific situation that feels unsafe. Therefore, it's important to think about in what mental state you want to be when you engage in sexual acts. Does it feel okay to do this while being intoxicated? Or is it more difficult to listen to your body and boundaries if you do so? Is a one-night stand okay for you? Or do you seek more connection before you allow someone to touch your body? And what about a kiss? If this okay with someone you just met, or do you need a little more time for it?

Yes, no, maybe list!

Grab your pen and three sheets of paper. Let's figure out which boundaries you have for yourself surrounding intimacy. Start with writing down of a 'yes' for things that excite you, make you feel tingling in your body or sound very interesting to you. Continue with a 'no' for the things that make you tense in a negative way, sound scary and dangerous to you, or are simply not of any interest. And finaly a 'maybe' for the things that sound exciting, but certain conditions to be met before you want to engage in them, or the things you simply are not sure about.

Think of behaviors, examples and situations and put them on one of the papers. Some themes for inspiration are: foreplay, locations, mental/emotional state, types of sex, types of partners, bodyparts, fantasies.

Keep in mind that this list does not have to be final! It's just for you to have a clear idea of what feels good to you before you find yourself in certain situations and have to make a decision on the spot.

I want to repeat that you have autonomy over your own body, which means that your 'no' is a complete sentence. You do not owe anyone an explanation on why this is a no, except when it feels right to you to have a conversation about it. It is not respectful behavior to convince someone who gave a 'no' into a 'yes'. We'll get into the topic of consent more later.

Talking about sex and boundaries can be scary, taboo or awkward. It's like stepping into a new territory. A way to make it less intense, can be to have this conversation with a friend first before diving into this topic with a potential sexual partner.. You can ask a friend whether they would be open to have a conversation about sexual boundaries. It is important to ask whether the other person is okay with this conversation since you do not know their experiences and triggers with this topic.

To make a conversation like this easier, you should make sure that the surroundings are right. Do you have the time to actually dive into the topic? Does everyone have the emotional and mental space to have this conversation? Are you somewhere where you can speak freely? Is there a mutual understanding that it is okay to express emotion if they raise? Do you have the tools to deal with potential triggers and fears? Are you willing to have a conversation where you witness each other in your truth, instead of trying to convince/safe/fix the other person? And lastly, agree that if it is too much for someone, it is okay to walk away to get some air or ask for the conversation to be paused until another moment.

Conversation starters that can be useful:

- *Do you feel okay kissing someone you just met?*
- *Which fantasies do you have?*
- *What is a firm boundary you have sexually and why?*
- *Which type of sex would you like to try?*
- *Is there a part of your body nobody is allowed to touch?*
- *Is there something that you are scared of sexually?*

Exploring your sexuality, desires and fantasies; but also your boundaries, fears and insecurities, can be empowering, exciting. It may boost your confidence to know what you like and dislike, give you some stability when you engage in sexual relationships. It may strengthen your relationship to yourself.

There are lots of forms of intimacy you can explore before having penetrative sex with a new, or current, partner. This helps create a safe foundation for the both of you to explore this aspect of your relationship.

—

In sexual encounters, there are many 'grey areas': where does consent end and co-ercion start? It's important to think about yourself, but also about how the person - or people- you share intimacy with feel. How do you show up for both of you. The 'survivor' role and 'perpetrator' role are not asigned to a gender. It's possible that you have been on both sides of the coin.

Now that we have a clear vision on what feels right for you in a sexual setting, it's good to set standards of how you want to show up. What type of standards do you want to hold yourself and others accountable for? What is important to you? In what ways do you want to make sure the other person feels safe?

In the last chapter we dove into what consent means, now it is good to create a clear view on how to work with this in real life situations. The situations where consent might be unclear for someone, can have massive consequences. Preventing sexual violence means understanding how to make sure that there is a clear consensual understanding at all times.

A big topic, or grey area, is if the people who engage in a sexual act are not aligned in their consent. Let's first of all understand that consent is an ongoing process. If someone says 'yes' to sex today, it does not mean that they say 'yes' to sex everyday from now on. However, even in a shorter timeframe, it can happen that someone consents to kissing, and the start of sexual engagement, but later feels a no, which results in rape. Consent is a delicate matter, and it is in no way the 'fault' of a victim. Consensual sex means a full body yes of all people involved at all times.

There are situations where people are not able to express their 'no' clearly, and situations in which a no gets overheard or ignored. These situations can have a combination of many reasons. We have the fact that there is a lot of performing in sexual encounters which prevents us from really listening to our body, or connect with the other person. We have the problem that switches in, or the lack of, consent get's overlooked with or without intention.

Intentional overlooking of the lack of consent is often rooted in rape culture, a problem we'll get into later. Or sometimes, people simply have bad intentions. The good and bad exist in all of us, and unfortunately there are people who do bad things.

The unintentional overlooking of consent can come from not understanding a silent, or subtle no. Not being able to listen to the other person can have many reasons. It's important to learn how to listen to your sexual partners body, energy, and words. Consent get's expressed in more ways than words. To truly listen, it's needed to connect to each other in a way where both are able to expres and receive consent during the whole interaction.

It's good to realize that it's okay to take a short break, feel whether there is still a yes or it turned into a no. It's okay to go slow, to stop and maybe not climax at all. It's okay to want to do specific sexual acts, and not do others. By slowing down, you learn the language of your body. However, it is in no way or form wrong to want more intense or fast sexual encounters, as long as there is a consensus about this.

Sex is a way to connect to another person on a deeper level, or can be a way to express and release. However, in today's world it oftentimes can turn into a performance due to the influence of Porn and Sex being so widely available and sold to us at all times.

It's important to understand our why in sexual connections, and to be clear, open and receiving for the other person. It can happen that we see the other person as a mean to our goal, which means that we see them as a body to climax with. This takes away the humanity and connection from the sexual acts and makes the situation more prone to sexual violence. This attitude goes against the tide of seeing each other as equal, of treating others as equal.

Ofcourse, there are situations in 'real life' where both people feel the desire to share this together: it might be in a one-night stand, or in a wild night in a couple or between friends. This brings us in a danger-zone: how do we make sure that it is consensual? How do we prevent overlooking each other's no? Does this fit in with your stance on how to have respectful sexual encounters?

Let me be very clear: I am not opposed to a wild night of sex, in contrast, if both people desire this it is a beautiful way to connect and release. However, it is important to understand with yourself how to keep all sexual encounters safe, and free of co-ercion.

I want to ask you to close your eyes, take some deep breaths and sink into the body. An easy way to do this is by focussing on deep, slow breaths in the belly. Once you feel connected to your body, ask yourself: why do I desire to have sexual encounters? And really feel whatever emotions and sensations come up in the body.

Afterwards, grab a pen and paper, and journal for 5-10 minutes on the next prompt:

How do I make sure there is continous consent whitin myself and my sexual partner?

Ofcourse, this is something we can't resolve in journalling about it for 5-10 minutes. But it does bring awareness to the way you show up for yourself and your sexual partner. Substances, emotions, frustration can influence the way we show up. But if we have a clear vision of our ethics in this, we always have something to come back to.

Grab a new paper, and take the time to write some agreements with yourself: How do you show up in a way where you are aware of your consent during a sexual encounter? How do you listen to your partner's consent? In what way will you make sure to create a safe space for both to express a yes and no?

These answers can ensure that you are able to act with integrity in your next encounters. Please be aware of the fact that consent is a journey. It might happen that you will not listen to your own no, or someone else's. This is painful, sad, but does not make you a monster unles you did this on purpose. In these situations, it is important to put the needs of the person whose boundaries were overridden in the front. To learn and heal from the situation and make amends if the survivor desires this.

Lastly, let's turn into the body one last time. Shake it out, dance for a few songs and when you are ready: sit down and take some deep breaths. Imagine you are in a sexual encounter and mid way you feel a no, visualize yourself saying this no and stopping the encounter, which emotions and sensations come up? Just write them all down without judging. When you've done this and you feel like you still have the space: visualize you in the other role. Mid-encounter your sexual partner tells you no, how does this make you feel? What do you need from yourself to be able to instantly accept this & create a safe space for the other?

This last feel in might bring a lot of emotions, sensations, worries and fear. Try to witness them instead of turning them stories. Emotions are often just there to be felt, and by doing this exercise you prepare yourself to work with boundaries in a 'real life' situation. If the experience is too overwhelming, give yourself time and space. Do something which sooths you: whether this is going for a long walk, asking a friend whether they have the time and space to talk it through, or seeking professional help.

It's important to understand how substances and societal norms influence us making these decisions. Our decisionmaking is not completely conscious and these influences make a big difference. By creating a clear vision on consensual sex first and being aware of the influence of each substance on your behavior, you can harnas yourself against unwanted experiences for both parties. Let's be clear that this is a short overview, if you want to dive into the substances you use deeper, there are many scientific articles explaining how it influences the brain, or spiritual explanations of what it does to your energetic field.

Alcohol changes our ability to judge danger and blocks our impulse control due to it's influence on the prefrontal cortex and GABA receptors. This can lead to the inability to read social cues, like a clear yes or no in a sexual setting. It also influences our root and sacral chakra, which leads to the inability to be centered or understand our desires. This makes it even harder to understand whether the yes we feel is ours, or an imposed yes.

Cannabis influences the CB1 receptors in our brain, which changes our perception, can heighthen our anxiety or make us dissociate from the body and situation. It can increase the risk of a freeze response or make us unaware of our bodily uncomfortablity. This can activate our third eye and numb the throat chakra, which leads to not being able to see the situation for what it is and express what we feel.

MDMA makes our brain explode with serotonin, oxytocin and dopamine, while simultaneously shutting down the amygdala. This can lead to euphoria and reduced fear. It is really hard in these moments to discern whether you actually feel a connection or it's just the drugs talking, the crash in hormones afterwards might lead to regret and realizations of rape. These drugs force an opening of our heart chakra and influences the solar plexus. Both of this leads to forced trust in others and a dissolving ability to see our own boundaries and act upon them.

Cocaine blocks the reuptake of dopamine and overstimulates the connections of reward in our brain. This can lead to an increase of confidence, impulsivity and risky behavior. This can result in being pushy or aggressive towards a sexual partner, or saying yes to things you do not actually want since you don't feel your actual fears. This activates our Solar Plexus and Root Chakra, which makes us very pushy and overdriven. This substance can overtake us, which might lead to ignoring other people's boundaries more easily.

Psychedelics disrupt our default mode network and heighten our sensory experiences. This can take away our ability to feel like we have autonomy over our body and the possibility to say no. Touch can feel way more intense, while losing your ability to consent. These types of substances may also make past experiences resurface, which can lead to intense emotions and feelings. This influences our Crown Chakra, which disconnects us from our body and the possibility to feel whether we want certain sexual encounters or not.

Ketamine can dissociate our mind and body, which lead to the inability to say yes or no, or feel our consent. Where GHB mimics GABA, which can lead to unconsciousness, which is why this is commonly used as a rape drug since the other person is not in a position to say yes or no, nor can they physically take action. Both of these disconnects us from our own energetic body, which takes away our possibility to fully consent and forces a surrendering response.

There is way more depth for how specific substances influence your physical body, your brain, your emotions, your energyfield. If you are a regular user of one of these substances, dive into this topic to understand in what ways you are paying the price for experiencing these substances.

After reading the influence of these substances on your system, it's time to reflect for yourself. Make a list of the substances you have used in the past or use frequently. If you have the names, answer the following questions for each substance:

How does the substance affect me and why do I use it?

In which ways does this influence my ability to understand my own and my partners yes or no in a sexual connection?

Do I want to engage in sexual acts while being influenced by this substance and under which conditions does it align with my morals surrounding consent?

This exercise it not meant to convince you to stop using certain substances, or point out how bad they are for you. Using substances is a personal choice, but one where it is necessary to be aware of it's influence. Using substances can come from a place where you enjoy it, or from a place of running away for your feelings and life.

If you feel that you might misuse substances, don't feel afraid to reach out for help. Just like around sexual violence, there are a lot of misconceptions surrounding addiction. Finding professional help, having a conversation with a friend or just reading about it online is a very brave step to be proud of. You never have to struggle alone, or hide these things. We are all human, and all of us to some degree struggle with the same problems.

—

Now, we gave attention to situations where both parties were able to expres their yes and no, whether it is with words or subtle. However, there are many situations where one of you will not be able to. This is not a mistake, or something we can blame ourselves of the other for. It's a natural reaction for any human to danger. Therefore, it is important to understand this.

One of the biggest misconceptions is 'They did not say no, so how can it be rape?'. Or idea that it is solely the responsibility of your sexual partner to protect their boundaries. Especially the argument 'I didn't know, so how can I be to blame?' misses the mark completely.

You've now made up your mind on what sexual violence is, you understand which standards you want to hold yourself for to have consensual sex, now it's time to imbed some 'real world' situations. Just like you are not always able to feel and express your yes or no, others aren't always able to as well. This is not their mistake, this is common knowledge we can take into consideration to have ethical and consensual sex. It gives us the possibility to take our responsibility to prevent sexual violence on a small level, which can one person at a time ripple to bigger effects.

Let's take a moment to reflect yourself first. Take a few moments to arrive in this moment. Once you feel present with yourself, write down the following misconception, followed by every emotion, thought, sensation that comes up when you contemplate on it for 10 minutes. Make sure to observe your thoughts, as well as your physical sensations.

"It is only my responsibility to say no"

Once you have done this, reflect whether this is the same asnwer you would have given if the question was: "It is solely my best friends respibility to say no" or "I am not responsible to protect the sexual boundaries of my partner".

And after this, sit with the question: "Can I think of situations where I will not be able to say no or protect my boundaries?"

Take your time to be with these questions, if it is enough for today put the book away and don't force yourself to work through these feelings and ideas more than you have the capacity to in this moment. Sexual violence is a heavy topic, and it is normal to feel negative emotions when we focus on it.

We need to understand the different responses to an unwanted experience. It's impossible to predict how you, or your sexual partner, will respond, since that differs based on your emotional, mental, physical state. But also variables like: your previous experiences, your relationship to the perpetrator, the setting you find yourself in, possible used substances, societal gender roles, expectations, cultural believes, the state of your Nervous-System.

It's very common to think 'but I would never experience something like that!' Or 'That person cannot be assaulted, they normally are so quick to respond'. Please understand that these are misconceptions. Everyone can fall victim to sexual violence. Sexual violence is possible without any physical aggression. Unconsensual sexual acts are everywhere. If we face a threath, there are common responses. Fight, Flight and Freeze are the most known, but there are also the concepts of Fawn and Flop. Here is a short overview of these responses:

Fight, the response where we use aggression (physical or verbal) as a reaction. This can look like yelling back at someone who makes a sexist joke, physically attacking someone who is abusing you.

Flight, the response where we make sure to get out of the situation. This can look like physically running away from a perpetrator, avoiding situations where sexual acts can happen.

Freeze, the response where we don't do anything at all. This can look like standing still while someone is harassing you, not being able to say no in a setting where sexual acts happen.

Fawn, the response where we try to please an abuser into not hurting us worse. This can look like sleeping with someone to prevent them from being aggressive, or laughing along with a comment that hurts us.

Flop, the response where we completely dissociate and our body becomes loose to prevent pain. This can look like you fainting during sexual assault, or your mind shutting down during moments of distress.

These are automatic responses, in which we do not make a conscious choice to behave that way. These responses can make us unable to take action to stop rape from happening, and this is nothing to be ashamed of or to carry the blame for. The guilt of sexual violence should be carried by the one perpetrating it, not the one experiencing it.

Therefore, I will not get into how to 'prevent' these responses from happening, since that is not the point at all. It's simply put a part of 'rape culture' to think that we have to make sure we don't have a trauma response to sexual violence. What is important, is for people to understand that consent is in subtle communication, and part of this is checking in regularly, being aware of possible inability of our sexual partner to say no.

With this knowledge of consent and the possible inability to communicate consent, it is important to think about ways you can listen to a sexual partner. Examples can be by communicating thoroughly prior to having sex, choosing a 'safe word', making sure to be present with subtle changes in behavior or expression, creating short pauses where you check in with each other.

Take a moment to sit in silence, think of yourself or a sexual partner feeling those responses. What precautions feel right to you to prevent this from happening? How do you want to show up when your sexual partner experiences this with you?

To truly enjoy sex, our nervous system needs to feel safe. This is a big topic, and this book only dips it's toes in the big ocean of scientific, somatic, spiritual knowledge and practices. For a deeper understanding to experience a nice and safe sexlife, to be able to explain what it takes to your close circle or even create a bigger change: I would urge you to find a source that excites you and dive into it! It can help you live a happier, freer, calmer, more conscious and enjoyable life.

I understand this last exercise might not statisfy you when you have experienced sexual violence before, and want to make sure this never happens again. I have been there too, in all of these responses, and for a long time I judged myself for it. There might be a whole fight in you, from wanting to act as if you have never been hurt, to running away from any type of discomfort, to wanting to make sure that it will never happen again.

Unfortunately, we can not ensure that we won't experience sexual violence again. We can bring balance back into ourselves by healing, which we will talk about later. We can get to know our own boundaries, learn our worth and expect others to treat us accordingly, we can even speak up about it. But the harsh truth is, some things are out of our control. There are people on this planet who will still hurt you, even if you have done everything 'right'. Someone raping you, has nothing to do with you, it has to do with their internal world.

As much as we like to believe that everything has a reason, and we can influence everything, sometimes it is wrong place, wrong time. We can't change someone else's heart, values, morals and behavior. All we can do is change ourselves and inspire others to do the same. This alone, shows why we as a society have to stand up together, we have to dive deep into our beliefs and change our attitude.

This last paragraph might leave you feel hopeless. However, I believe that you diving into this topic, and having the resources to do so is already proof that there is hope. In a lot of countries, violence is no longer a prerequisite for criminal rape, it is consent. There are many people and organisations standing up, demanding attention, legal support and active change for the problem that is sexual violence. Slowly, but surely, we get into a change of society by addressing 'rape culture'

But before we go there, I want to applaud you for making it this far through the book. This topic is painful, and I'm sure you realized some things you would rather not face. You taking back control over your body, is an act of rebellion in a world where we get discouraged to do so. You facing the subconscious thoughts, in order to have safe joyful sex, is an act of bravery in itself. The feeling of owning your body, taking back full autonomy over yourself? One of the most beautiful lessons learned. So thank you, for changing this world one heart at the time.

—

Sexual violence is way broader than rape, unwanted touching. Therefore, getting to know your bodily pleasures and sexual boundaries is nothing more or less than a great start. In the previous chapter, we've covered what sexual violence and consent is, but also your moral stance surrounding this topic. Now it's time to see where it shows up in your life. To look further than rape, and work our way down into the root of this problem. To look at believes you inherited, ideas you haven't thought through, behaviors you don't think about.

To prevent sexual violence, we have to dive deep into societal and cultural norms. It's not a closed container where sexual violence happens. Unfortunately, the precursors are woven through our daily life. A comment about how 'she is asking for sex'. The shrug of your shoulders when you see someone in power touch another person unwanted. The idea that a man being touched by a woman is sexy and wanted. The fake smile along with the sexist joke. That conversation with a friend about how you'll have sex with your partner tonight 'just to keep them happy'.

But also in the conversation with your friend debating whether she has enough proof go to report rape. Or in the warning to men for false accusations. It shows in how a police officer does not take your complaint about someone touching your but in public serious. You can find it in the believe that a man has to 'win over' a woman and make the first moves. Or in the idea that a male partner always wants sex, and can never be raped.

Diving into those things might be painful. It's important to be completely honest with yourself, to not judge but just observe. You probably have made mistakes in the past that enabled sexual violence. I know for a fact that I did, and it was not untill I looked into it that I was able to change this. Take this part easy, allow yourself to look at your mistakes without punishing yourself. It's more important to learn from them & not repeat them again. If this puts you into a dark spiral, ask for help. You are human and we all make mistakes. It's brave to repair them or try to do better. There is nothing to be ashamed for. Having those conversations with a loved one or professional can give both parties new perspectives and lessons.

To further understand how we can prevent sexual violence, it's important to understand the term 'rape culture'. The UN women explains this as: *"Rape culture is the social environment that allows sexual violence to be normalized and justified, fueled by the persistent gender inequalities and attitudes about gender and sexuality. Naming it is the first step to dismantling rape culture."*[42] Let's break this down again.

Rape culture refers to communities where sexual violence is normalized and justified. Before you say that in your country this is not the case, or in your direct environment you are too modern for this, take a minute to truly think about it. And be realistic: one in three women experiences sexual or physical abuse, are you really the exception? Don't get me wrong, I wish for everyone to be the exception. But we can only change what we dare to face.

Normalizing sexual violence, means that it doesn't shock you anymore to hear it. It turns into an everyday thing. How often do you hear about sexual violence or rape? Does it make

---

[42] UN Women. (n.d.). *Take action: 10 ways you can help end violence against women* [Explainer]. https://www.unwomen.org/en/articles/explainer/take-action-10-ways-you-can-help-end-violence-against-women

you angry, or do you believe it's part of life? Part of normalizing is not even recognizing behavior as such. It's not having a clear vision of what is right and what is wrong, and therefore accepting unjust behavior.

Normalizing can be in direct behavior: waving someones concernes away with 'overreacting' or simply saying that the situation is the way it is. It can be seen in the presumption that if intimacy was not violent, it cannot be rape. Laughing at cat-calling on the streets, portraying it as a form of complimenting. An institution or company wanting to sweep sexual violence under the rug, to protect their reputation.

Normalizing can also be seen in indirect behavior, like teaching girls self-defence and focussing on 'how not to get raped' instead of focussing on 'don't rape'. Assuming that since someone had sex with multiple people before, they want to sleep around consistently. Movies ideolizing the persistance of someone to sleep with you, instead of accepting a no. Policies which focus on working with the aftermath of sexual violence instead of preventing it.

Justifying sexual violence, is shown in your first thoughts when you hear about it. Do you question whether you believe someone? Do you feel the need to look at the motive and intention of the perpetrator? Or are you more interested in the 'mistakes' on the side of the victim? Let me be very clear on this last question: nobody deserves to be blamed for experiencing sexual violence. Part of justifying sexual violence comes from the fact that looking at the truth can be too confrontational with truths we lived ourselves.

A direct form of justification is victimblaming: 'they drank alcohol and wore a revealing dress, they were asking for it!'. Or Media/the justice system looking at the perpetrators potential over the harm affecting the survivor's life. A very clear justification is laughing at comments, stating 'it's just a joke!' Or pointing out: "well we kissed before, how should I know they did not want to have sex?" Which assumes that consent is a one time decision instead of an ongoing communication.

Justification also happens indirectly: Pointing out someone's redemption for their behavior, instead of looking at the effects it had. Stating how playing 'hard to get' is just the way to get someone in your bed, or believing that one cannot rape another human being in a marriage. Or the downplaying of lived experiences, by calling it 'out of hand' or 'fantasies' instead of the violence showed in reality. Lastly, we see the justification in accepting power imbalances and double standards for gender.

This normalization and justification is: *"fueled by the persistent gender inequalities and attitudes about gender and sexuality."* Simply stated: by the believe that the genders are not equal and certain attitudes with regards to gender and sexuality. Simple examples? The idea that men who sleep with a lot of people are 'cool', but women who do the same are seen as 'sluts'. Or the vision that a man has to perform, and be dominant in bed; where a woman should be submissive and allow someone to 'take' her. Or the idea that a man should always want sex, and therefore cannot experience sexual violence.

It is an inescapable truth that there are differences in the different genders we have. But it is learned behavior to put a 'value' to these differences, make it into a competition. It is human to form opinions on sexuality, but our opinion of someone else is just a reflection of our own fear and insecurity.

Unfortunately even today, in 2025, there is still an imbalance between men and women, and a preference for 'cis-gendered hetero' sex. This imbalance is seen in the 9-to-5 lifestyle which works perfect for the hormonal cycle of a men, but not for the 28-day cycle of a women. Or the pay-gap we still see in jobs, the harrasment some women have to accept to keep their job and income. The fact that there is still a male dominance a lot of industries and leadership positions.

We face harmful stereotypes for men and women. Sometimes even resulting in the idea that men are entitled to the female body and unable to withhold their urges. Which puts pressure and heaviness on both genders. The stigma's around sexuality: 'gay man always want sex' and the fetishization of virginity and race make this problem even more layered.

To be able to dismantle rape-culture, it is important to understand and change the beliefs you have. This can lead to changing subconscious behaviors. We have to understand the way it is imbedded in ourselves, before we can bring a change in society. By slowly unpacking this, you can open up that conversation with those around you. After this, broaden it to standing up in unjust situations that happen in front of us. Hopefully, this might lead to changes in policies, law and reality.

it for some moments, you can write down whatever came up for you.

- *Men and women are equal to each other*
- *I am allowed and safe to express my sexuality and boundaries*
- *Those around me listen if I reach out for help*

If any of these statements brought up intense feelings, allow yourself to sit with them. However, please don't drown in them! Reach out for support if it is too much to bear.

This exercise might have given you a clear overview of what 'undercover' forms of sexual violence there are around you. But I would love to give some more examples, for you to just have a think whether it is okay or not for you.

The saying 'Boys will be Boys' as a response to a man touching a women's but in a café without consent. Or as a response to a 'jokingly said' sexist comment like 'Look at her short skirt, she is asking for it!'

The deeply imbedded idea that men are worth more than women. Showcased in how some strict forms of religions as christianity and Islam. For example the fact that in some religious political parties, women are not allowed to be chosen to run for election in the house of representatives in the Netherlands. The overruling of Abortion Rights in the USA, making a huge impairment in the bodily autonomy of Women. Honor killings in cultures to 'protect' a family, and the huge problems of 'femicide' in a lot of countries where women are targetted simply for being a woman. But also the precursion of a woman having money because of her dad/her husband or simply to get a high-paying job.

The huge problem of sextrafficking we still have on the planet. Children, women and men being sold to work in the sex industry. Sex seen as a 'need' and people who have to 'serve'. This is an example of the dark side of the sex industry, there are absolutely ethical forms of sex work with people who consciously and consensualy choose to do this job.

Sex being shown as something easy accessible, and coercion being romantisized in movies. Laughing about receiving an un-asked for sexual picture online. The marketing idea of 'sex sells'. Or the forwarding of nudes to our friends 'because they made the pictures themselves right?' Or the idea that watching porn daily is 'nothing to worry about' and sexualizing pictures of young children is 'okay'. The sharing of intimate details of someone else's sexlife, or gossiping about each other's sexual adventures.

And the idea that you are only a 'man' if you have regular sex and can flirt with many women, or women only kissing another women to get the attention of a men. The bragging about sleeping with a lot of people, or hyping each other up to 'score'.

The lack of conversations about sex, and therefore people doing what they think is 'normal' instead of learning what feels right. For example someone who has been married for a long time and has sex regularly 'because that's what you are supposed to do'. Or someone who learned about sex through porn and expecting their sex life to be such a performance as well.

These examples give a clear overview of how rape-culture is interwoven with the way we live. By keeping it this way, we enable people to use sexual violence. We stay in this loop of hurt and pain. To prevent sexual violence, we have to change the root of this behavior and change the narrative. We have to start by changing our direct environment, and hopefully influence a bigger society with a ripple effect. Ofcourse, activism and influencing the legal system plays a part as well, we will get into this soon.

Having clarity on what rape-culture is and how it affects us, it is important to dive deeper into the root. Because where awareness is the first step, understanding the cause of a problem is the only way to actually change it. What do you think causes you to think this way? What pain is underneath this way of acting by all of us?

So let's take a moment once again! Shake it out first, go for a walk and make sure that your mental clutter is minimalized. When you are so far, write out for yourself in 2 sentences what rape-culture is. Once you've done this, elaborate why you think this phenomenon is alive, what causes people to behave this way?

—

Sexual violence hurts both men and women, and there are male victims of sexual violence. Their pain is just as valid and important as that of women. As stated before, the guilt of sexual violence lays by the perpetrator. The taboo for male victims, and the prejudice that a man can not fall victim to sexual abuse is a harmful lie.

It is however a fact that women proportionally speaking are the biggest group of survivors of sexual abuse. Therefore, in the why behind sexual violence and rape culture, there is extra attention for the unequal treatment of men and women.

Speaking about it in this way, does not mean that the pain of male victims is overlooked or invalid. That being said, we'll dive into possble roots for Rape Culture and the global enabling of sexual violence.

Primarely, the idea that men are stronger than women, and are entitled to take what they desire. Rape culture is not just an idea, or a theory, it's the world we live in sustained by a system that is rooted in patriarchy. Patriarchy has become a taboo topic. With opinions variating from not believing this is still happening, and it's just an angry women thing to pure rage against men for dominating women it's tough to find middle ground.

It is a fact, that underlying ideas as male are the dominant species keep the system of rape culture intact. The, unconscious, objectification of women does the same. This objectification can be done by men as seeing women as objects for pleasure, but also by women using their beauty to manipulate a situation. The unhealthy stereotypes that are engraved in our brains by society help keep these systems alive. A very simple reason for complying with this, is that we get rooted in comfortability. It is easier to comply with what we know, than create something new. This resistance can be rooted in fear and nostalgia.

If you look at society, we can see that even in policies and insitutions there is enabling of the current situation. Even now, in 2025, there is a wage-gap between men and women. And a significant bigger amount of men in positions of power. If a survivor speaks up, there is a high chance of public shaming. On top of that, there is a low convictionrate for rape, not even speaking of the amount of victims who get waved away while reporting a crime or never get to the point to actually do this. When someone steps forward to bring a change, they face a lot of resistance.

The reasons rooted in sociology for this can be found in for example power and control dynamics. Keeping the situation as it is, brings forward an opportunity to control society. Using these dynamics, it is easier to gain control. We have normalized sexual violence so much, we don't fully see it as a problem anymore. We grew up with so many narratives around this topic, it takes a lot of time to unlearn it. Starting to change the way you view the world, might make you feel vulnerable and ungrounded.

In spirituality, we can find -wrongful?- interpretations of how men are superior to women. We all know the stories of religious institutions covering-up sexual violence. There is also the false narrative that this had a meaning, sexual violence is part of a plan to teach you a lesson. There is a focus on peace, which can force forgiveness and lead to spiritual bypassing. In the search for meaning, we can tell ourselves all kind of stories of why it is okay.

The biggest question we have to ask ourselves, is the comfort of staying the same worth the price we pay for this? Are we more afraid of new things that come from creating a new system without rape culture, or does the pain caused by this system outweigh the fear?

On a personal level, we can explain this in the following way: sometimes we need to hurt a lot once, to prevent hurting a little bit continiously. We need to stand so strong in our desire for change, that we can convince others to take this leap of faith with us.

Make a list with reasons why we should keep the situation the same, and another list with reasons for change. Find your own stance in this, including reasoning why it is time to overthrow rape culture. How you take action accordingly is up to you, but this will give you the clarity you need for your personal choice.

—

Everyone fights sexual violence in their own way. For some, slowly healing themselves is the biggest fight in itself. For others it is joining protests. Speaking up at a family party when someone makes an enabling comment. Listening to a friend share their heartbreaking story. Writing a letter to your government, pointing out hurtful truths. Making video's for social media. Becoming a therapist, or start holding space in a different healing modality. Educating young people at schools, having a conversation with a colleague. Writing a book. Every form of prevention is a valuable step towards a world where sexual violence doesn't exist anymore.

If you are ready to do something for the world, from a place of love: we need you. However, it is important to always make sure that you are okay first. Losing yourself in supporting others is not helping, it is harming you. Remember the example of an emergency in a plane: prior to helping the people around you, you need to put your own oxygenmask on! Yes, the world needs you, but we need you to look after yourself first. Making sure that you find your way back to a balanced place and don't hurt others is already a big step.

Preventing sexual violence starts small: by actively listening to a friend sharing their story, and responding without prejudgements and in an empowering way. By stopping your colleague from making a hurtful comment. Through stepping in when you see a dangerous situation. By reporting your abuse to the police. In sharing your story openly, creating space for others to open up as well. Raise children who condemn rape culture. Having the hard, awkward conversations with others to make sure they understand what sexual violence is, and how to stop it. Every act can be a pivotol change in someone else's life!

If you have the resources, find a local shelter where survivors can get care and help out. Or support a political movement like Every Women Treaty with a donation, so they can continue their fight for change. Share the NGO that you align with in your direct environment, asking them to support this cause as well. Volunteer at organizations that are fighting sexual violence, use your unique skills and talents! Give someone who is currently fighting their abuser in court money for their legal bills, or a free meal to lighten their day. Share your wealth with those in need, in the form of time, money and resources.

To fully stop this cycle, we need a change in legal policies. This can start small with your companies working conditions.

Calling out the negative impact specific policies has for the position of a victim. Boycotting specific companies or calling them out for enabling abuse. Fighting for equality rights, for changes in criminal law where rape means unconsensual instead of forced. We need clarity in what sexual violence is, and why we want to stand together against it. We need to vote for those politicians who are ready to take a stance. We need to become the ones who make the world ready for a change, and back up those who take a leap of faith and start creating change in their own way.

But most of all: we need a change in the actual world. We need police officers to understand what it means to get violated, and act with grace towards someone who speaks up. We need judges to take a survivor seriously, and put their needs before the perpetrators without doing it from a place of hate. We need to start conversations in community and at schools to educate people on this topic. We need to make resources accessible: in every language and for low costs. We need to help those taking action to generate money, so they can keep up the good work. We need to spread a message loud and clear.

It is our job to flip the script. To change the narrative from 'how can we protect' to 'what does it take to stop'. Where it is incredibly important for everyone to learn how to harnass themselves and those around them for sexual violence, this is not the main goal. It is important to understand why sexual violence is not okay, and we should never condone anything that enables this, nor should we perpetrate sexual violence. It's time to teach people not to touch others unconsensually. This is the only way to really stop this terrible problem. The world to understand that this behavior is not okay, nor will any excuse make it okay. And for everyone to make the decision, each day, not to hurt anyone else.

In what ways are you ready to take action? Take a moment to write down all your talents and qualities. How can you use these to make the world free of sexual violence? How can you use your joy, to bring love in the world? In what ways will your voice make an impact? Which privileges you have can make a change, to stand up for those who are currently suffering?

Find your way to create political pressure to bring change into the system.

Use your voice to educate others.

Make the protest you attend into a party with your pressence.

Stand with those who are creating change, give them support.

Use your creativity to make art that speaks loud and clear.

Make sure to pour from a full cup, to only give when you have time and resources enough to help yourself first. Do it from a balanced place, not blind anger.

I want to conclude with one thing: this work is a labour of love. A labour of love for the person who never deserved to live this pain. A labour of love for those who deserve to not have to face a cruel world. A labour of love for those who believe in change. A labour of love for yourself. A labour of love for the world.

Nadine Donselaar

From now on:

Let's call it how it is: they raped them.

It's time to put the shame and guilt back where they belong,

To give the burden back to those with wandering hands.

For so long we've normalized, justified,

Because it happens to almost all of us at some point, right?

We're done now, my body, my rules

Nobody get's to touch it, without an enthusiastic, full body yes.

It might sound inconvenient, to those not ready to face their own desires

Scary even, to those not willing to take up responsibility

Victims have carried the weight for long enough,

Focussing on how never to repeat this cruelty

It's time to flip the coin,

The focus on why we don't want to perpetrate

***

Will you ever heal?

When I first started talking about Sexual Violence, I got asked the question 'did you heal?' many times. Sexual violence caused me to get diagnosed with PTSD, I've physically struggled with endometrioses, pcos, a dys-regulated nervous system. We've probably all heard that trauma sits in the body, but the better I feel, the more I see it's little hands everywhere.

In the way I respond to my friends jokes, my career choices, the way I show up in romantic relationships, my -lack of- sexual desires, my political views, the way I proces emotions, the way I perceive the world, everywhere. After years of physical, energetical, mental, emotional, societal healing work. I've found my answer to the question.

I never 'healed', because that version of me was never meant to be 'fixed'. I became a happier, freer, healthier, calmer, more confident version of who she ever was. Yes, sometimes it still pops up, a flashback, behavioral patterns, physical discomfort. But it does not ruin my whole day, it affects me just a few minutes. I've learned to see the pain as a beautiful lesson instead of a heavy burden.

Don't get me wrong. I will never condone sexual violence, nor do I agree with 'what does not kill you makes you stronger'. It was not the pain I endured that made me strong.

The opposite, it was sitting with it and allowing myself to crumble underneath it's weight, my own consistent work, even when I felt scared and alone, slowly allowing close friends and family in: that turned me into a 'strong' woman. Strong in my eyes means soft, approachable, with a big heart, but clear not to cross any line with me.

You might be reading this and think "I've never been raped, I don't need to heal from sexual violence!" Still, I would like to ask all of you, every gender, to take a moment and dive into the discomfort that lives inside of you due to Sexual Violence.

There is shame, anger, stress, pain in all of us, not matter our gender. It's a fact that sexual violence does directly affect women more than man. However, other genders also experience sexual violence. And the indirect effects of this global disease can be found in as good as anyone.

In this chapter, we'll touch on different techniques and healing methods. Working through a painful topic like this can bring up old pain and trauma. It's a very brave decision to sit with yourself and actively help yourself to feel better. Congratulations on making this decision! Work like this, does not have to be done alone.

There are amazing specialists who can help you: Psychologists specialized in sexual trauma, Somatic Therapist, Energy Healers, Coaches. Make sure to always find someone who feels right and safe for you. Someone who communicates in a way you understand, who has knowledge of the complexities of trauma. Also someone who meets you where you are, who gives you the tools and walks besides you. You have all the knowledge and wisdom inside of you, you deserve guidance to find these answers instead of the text book perfect ones.

Healing is done in connection. It's a privilege to have family members or friends with who you can talk about these topics. If you have never done this, and feel the need to you can always start by asking them whether they would be open to have a conversation on this topic. If that scares you, imagine how you would act if the situation is reversed. If you have no-one to talk to, you are always welcome to contact me.

It is not your fault, to have experienced sexual violence. The shame is on the person who behaves poorly, not on the one who survives is. And if you have perpetrated someone, it is never too late to learn from it and make sure to, respectfully, make up for it. Even if that is in making sure you will never do this to someone else.

A lesson I personally learned while writing this book, after ten years of healing, was: I have never been broken and my story is not a burden. If anything, it thaught me lessons which I will forever cherish. That does not mean I owe those who've hurt me a thank you, I never deserved to learn lessons in such a harsh way.

May this journey of healing be a journey of getting to know yourself. Everytime a step closer towards a life ful of joy. There might be periods where you feel amazing, set-backs, moments where you feel triggered again. That's all okay. You are doing this for yourself, you don't have to perform, or hide behind a smile. Let's be brutally honest with ourselves and find joy in the journey.

Grab a pen and paper, set a timer for 5-10 minutes and answer the following prompt:

How has Sexual Violence directly or indirectly affected me?

Healing starts with awareness. Journaling on a topic can give us great insights. Journaling can showcase your thoughts, the stories you tell yourself, your behavioral patterns. By journalling with a timer of 5-10 minutes, you allow yourself to write without overthinking it. If you journal and think about something for a longer time, you get to know your thought process.

While having a clear overview of your current reality, it can be good to dive even deeper in the way sexual violence is present. *Read back* your answer on the way sexual violence affects you. To get more clarity, you can dive into these follow-up questions:

Which effect does it have on my physical body?

How does it affect my mind?

Which effect does it have on my emotions?

How does it affect my relationships?

Which effect does it have on my perception of the world?

How does it affect my behavior? Does it influence the choices that I make?

If you have answered all these questions, it might be good to put the book away for a little and go for a walk outside, take a shower, have a danceparty with yourself or call a friend. Clarity often comes with time. Give yourself the space to proces what you just did. It can happen that past experiences come up now. You are not crazy if these stories play in your head: reach out for help to a trusted person. Be aware of how you feel when you take some time to rest. Which sensations do you feel in your body? Which emotions come up in the next days?

Sexual violence, in all it's forms and even indirectly, can have many effects on you. I will give an non-exhaustive list of examples. Please understand that the experience and aftermath variate for everyone. You have your own unique story, which is not measured in how much you suffer. Your pain is valid, you don't have to prove it to anyone. It is possible that the effects you experience are different than those described, or maybe you only experience one: that does not make your suffering less valid.

Sexual violence can have the direct effect of bruises, an STD, or other physical wounds caused by the attack. Experiencing sexual violence can also lead to chronic pain, for example regular headaches due to stress, pelvic floor malfunction, vaginismus, fybromalgia, or even neurological disorders which cause you to have a different perception of pain and stress.

Violence can lead to a chronic state of stress, or a dysregulated nervous system. You can get so used to living in 'fight-or-flight' that you will not even notice these effects anymore. Living with a lot of stress can cause auto-immune disseases and allergies. Sometimes, sexual violence leads to inexplicable illnessess or symptoms. Hormonal disbalance, especially in women, can be a response to sexual violence. And lastly, being overly tired is a very common problem. An amazing book explaining how the physical body gets influenced by trauma is: the body keeps the score of Bessel van der Kolk.

Some of the biggest emotions that come up after sexual violence is shame and guilt. The feeling of being gross, like something has been taken away from you. The idea that it was your mistake, the guilt of 'allowing' it to happen to you (which is not fair!). There is also a feeling of isolation, that comes with the shame and guilt, of not being able to express this pain to others. Of having to carry this load alone.

Rage, pure anger and maybe even hatred that comes out as a volcano is another natural emotional response. Maybe towards the perpetrator, towards a loved one who says something wrong or just simply another person who is in the wrong place at the wrong time. Fear, grieve, sadness, emotional exhaustion are all common emotions as well.

Sexual violence can lead to C-PTSD or PTSD depending on the form of violence. Sexual abuse actually has the highest percentage of leading to ptsd from all forms of abuse. This has symptoms like anxiety, self-destructive behavior, difficulties to sleep and concentrate, violent outbursts. Sexual violence can increase the risk of self-harm and suicide. But also feeling of worthlessness, incapable of handling emotions, difficulty in connecting with others or creating relationships.

Cognitive functions like memory and clarity can be affected by this abuse. It can lead to brain fog, loss of memory and dissociation from the body and present moment. To cope with symptoms, addiction to substances, work, pain, or even sex can occur. An amazing author to find information on the effects of trauma is Dr. Gabor Maté.

Sexual violence can cause you, or those around you, to behave differently than you would normally do. Use of substances as a form of numbing is the first sign. Avoiding specific locations, sensations, people can be another way of changing behavior. Sometimes victims seek to be in a similar situation to re-enact the traumatic event, hoping to gain back control.

It can show up in intimate relationships as well. In romantic or sexual relationships, it affects the way you show up in the bedroom. From fearing sex, having flashbacks during, difficulties relaxing and orgasming to having compulsive sexual desires or intrusive sexual thoughts. It possibly leads you to emotional break-downs during sexual connection, or shutting down completely.

Shame and guilt can cause you to completely isolate from friends and family, you might stop opening up, sharing your emotions, having the ability to have an intimate conversation. Possible reckless behavior might push away those who love you. It can cause you to lose the ability to trust others, leaving you alone and afraid. It can also push you into hyper-independence, feeling the need to prove your worth through educational or career oriented goals. A hyper-focus on specific goals might lead to abandon those in your close circle.

Anger-issues or uncontrolled emotions can lead you to behave differently or hurtful towards those you love. Which can cause a drift in your relationships. The polar-opposite, people-pleasing, can lead to you slowly resenting those around you or feeling used.

Lastly, sexual violence can cause you to not think about the future. It can take away your perspective of living a long life, which results in you not taking the responsibility for your life. You might never want to make a 5-year plan, simply because you don't plan to live this long. This can cause a drift in your close relationships, since they worry about your wellbeing. Or simply leave you in difficult situations since you haven't prepared the practicalities or financial funds in a way that was necessary.

Sexual violence can close you off spiritualy. It can lead to the question: 'How can god exist if terrible things like this happen?' It might drift you away from religion, or spiritual practices. It might even make you feel like it is all bullshit. Or it can do the opposite, causing you to run towards spirituality in order to 'fix' you. Believing that you have to seek forgiveness from god, or redempt your worth through religious or spiritual practices.

The feelings of shame and guilt, or the idea that something took away part of your worth might lead to you feeling distant from god, love, the source or what it is you believe in. It can cause a spiritual crisis doubting the purpose of life. Which might result in you desperately trying to prove your worth, doing well. Or the opposite, in not caring at all about morals since you feel worthless to begin with.

One can spiral into the question: 'why did this happen to me?' Desperately seeking an answer in ideas like past lives and karma, believing that you caused this yourself. Seeking a purpose in the pain, a lesson. It can even lead to explanations why the survivor 'deserved' the pain.

Besides our physical body, we have an energetical body. My favorite book explaining this is Eastern Body, Western

Mind by Anodea Judith. If you prefer a scientific approach, Becoming Supernatural from Dr. Joe Dispenza might be better for you. Some examples are the Chakra System from the Hindu/Yogic traditions; the Meridians from Traditional Chinese Medicine; The Luminous Energy Field from Inca Shamanism; Sacred Geometry; The Rainbow Body from Tibetan Buddhism; The Ka from Ancient Egypt and many more examples like chi, prana, energy.

All these systems are beautiful in their own way, find something that speaks to you and start by understanding this. If this does not speak to you at all, don't force it. If it's meant to be, you will start working with it at some point.

The energetic body gets influenced by sexual violence as well. It can lead to gaps or distortion in the Aura (field of energy surrounding your physical body). This influences your mental, physical and emotional functions. It also influences the things you attract in your life. These experiences can create an unwanted connection between you and the perpetrator. A connection like this influences your energylevel, your emotions, your feeling of worth.

Personally, I prefer the Chakra System, which is why I'll use this in this book. Therefore we work with the seven main chakra's, which are 'energy wheels'. Specific spots in your body -along the spine- that impact our physical body, emotions, life and wellbeing. All seven correlate with different themes in our life.

The Root Chakra (Muladhara) focuses mainly on our feeling of being safe and centered. Sexual violence can cause us to not feel safe and dissociate from our body. The Sacral Chakra (Svadishtana) is our center of creation and emotions. Sexual violence can lead to guilt and shame, breaking the connection to our pleasure. Simultaneously it can cause us to be prone to addiction and compulsive sexual behavior. The Solar Plexus (Manipura) is our power-center, the place where we understand who we are. Sexual violence can lead to doubting our worth and people please for validation, or get overconfident and control others possibly even in an agressive way.

The Heart Chakra (Anahata) is the middle of our chakra system, it's the center of connection, love and trust. Sexual violence can disrupt our possibility to create relationships by shutting down. Or it can force connection through excessive empathy and putting our faith in the hands of others.

Our Throath Chakra (Vishuddhi) is the wheel of truth and expression, which makes us speak up for what we believe in. Sexual violence can shut down this center, causing us to have trouble expressing ourself due to unexpressed rage. Or it can make us explosive, overexplain ourselves constantly. Our Third Eye (Ajna) is the place that shapes our perception of the world. Sexual violence can cause us to not trust our intuition anymore, or suffer from vivid nightmares and dissociate from reality. Our Crown (Sahasrara) is the place that connects us with all there is. Sexual violence can cause us to completely feel isolated from love and god; or shut down the body and dissociate into space without feeling as if one lives on the planet.

These are absolutely an non-exhaustive list of trouble sexual violence can cause us energetically. They are simplified examples. These energetical problems can show up in our day-to-day life through physical, practical, emotional, and mental problems.

I do want to point out that problems that occur in our life can have many reasons. Not everything on this list solely has to be rooted in sexual violence. It can be that you are overly tired because of your job, and working through trauma at the same time.

Seeing a list like this might be intense and overwhelming. I understand that having awareness of how your life has been affected can make it feel unbearable and hopeless. You are allowed to feel this way, you are allowed to sit in bed for an hour to cry. You might want to throw this book away and ignore the world for a bit. Please, reach out for support to loved ones or a professional if needed. Don't struggle alone.

Awareness is the first, and most painful step towards healing, towards a life full of joy. Yes, your brain and nervous system might be rewired due to trauma. But the beautiful thing about your brain and body? You can rewire it again as many times as you want! However, you are not a problem to be fixed, you are a person with painful human experiences. Be soft with yourself, allow yourself to be just however you need to be. Understand that where working towards a goal of feeling in a different way is beautiful, sometimes we just need to feel all the feelings we have surpressed first.

Healing will never be a linear line. Some days you will feel the happiest ever, and another day the same pain might pop up again in a different way. This is exactly what life is about: we have the opportunity to learn from the same problem over and over again in different ways. And that's okay, you are here to experience the entirity of the human experience, not just happiness. There will be times where you won't do anything to feel better and just live your life, there will be times where you have a daily sadhana and dive deep into practices: both is perfect. Laughing at silly jokes with a friend and dancing around can be medicine as much as sitting in silence somewhere in nature with a spiritual guide doing an elaborate ceremony, as well as doing a full health check-up at a medical specialist.

In this book, I will pay attention to healing in a holistic way. As a Reiki Master, Kundalini Yoga Teacher, Oracle, Spaceholder, that's my forté. But before this, I want to bring up the importance of understanding the role of holistic health and spiritual well-being. Incorporating different modalities is beautiful and can create miracles in your life. However, working with a Psychotherapist specialized in Trauma Therapy might be what you need first. Taking rest, eating healthy is just as important as going to a doctor when you have physical problems.

I want to stretch how important it is to find the right support. If you are facing severe PTSD symptoms, a schooled professional is the right call. Alternative, or holistic, healing, or even a spiritual coach can absolutely help you, but we have to be aware of the fact that this is a different container of support, which is not always suitable. Energy healings can support our bodies to heal, alternative medicine battles physical illnesses in an amazing way. However, in specific cases you will need to go to the hospital or a doctor, and that's okay.

Alternative, and classic ways of support go hand in hand. They answer to different questions of support. You can use them simultaneously, since battling problems from multiple angles will support your process. But remember that rest, having space to be, not working on a specific goal is healing as well.

Your process of finding balance, finding joy, is your process. Do the things that feel right, dive into topics that interest you. Just because EMDR works for someone else, does not mean that it works for you. Going to Peru for an Ayahuasca ceremony is beautiful, if it feels right to you and not because it's a 'trend'. If you prefer going for a long walk instead of spending an hour on your yogamat: that's perfect. This is your journey, the only thing you really have to listen to is your heart and your body. So pick and choose between all the practices, ideas, ways of healing I will explain here and that you might come across. There is no 'set path', no 'obligation', just you finding what works for you and staying true to yourself.

After this much information, it's time to let it sink for a little bit and stop thinking. Maybe you can go for a walk, dance around. Set yourself a nice cup of tea. Once you are ready, it's time to reconnect with the body in the present moment. Make sure to have enough time for yourself to sink into this moment, without being interrupted by others or your phone.

Please be aware that when we start reconnecting with the body, it will not always be immediate relaxation. For some people, your brain will start racing, for others emotions will come up, or you will just find yourself bored or you might fall asleep. These are all natural reactions, it's a matter of trial and error to find what works for you and in which moments. Sometimes we need a good workout, other times we need a deep meditation: two different means to the same cause!

When you feel ready, I invite you to come into Balasana (Childspose) by kneeling down on the floor, get to a table top position (sitting on hands + knees) and slowly get down again resting the hips on the heels and bringing your forehead to the floor. There are different variations you can do: keeping the knees closed, touching together, or opening the knees and hips, resting in between the legs with the forehead on the floor. The arms can go overhead, with the palms touching the floor, you can put your hands underneath your head, or bring them back next to your body, with the palms up. Find the version of this that feels best to you. When you are here, try to simply observe the breath: is it deep or shallow, fast or slow, rhytmic or chaotic? Stay in this position as long as it feels good.

When you get out of this position, feel whatever is right for you. Start by writing down what you felt in this position. Afterwards, maybe you feel like you need a good shake to release all that came up, maybe you want to give yourself a big hug, maybe a long shower, making a delicious lunch, screaming into a pillow, doing a long meditation, having a loving chat with a friend: do what your body calls for.

From this place of balance, we will dive into what is alive in your body in this moment surrounding sexual violence. If you feel like that's too much right now, please postpone this to another moment. This is your journey and you need to do what is right for you.

We will get into Supta Baddha Konasana (Reclined Butterfly Pose). Grab some pillows to make it more comfortable for yourself, if you have it you can also grab a scarf or yogastrap. Start in a seated position. I'll invite you to bring the soles of your feet together, making a diamond shape with your legs. Slowly, but surely lay down on your back. To make this easier, you can use two pillows underneath your knees to support your legs and hips. You can put a pillow underneath your spine to help your back relax, make sure to put it 5-10 centimeters behind your bum, not immediatly touching. If you have a scarf or yogastrap, you can put it around you: covering the lower back and then circling around your feet, this will help open your hips and relax into the pose.

When you lay down, focus on your breathing again. It's good to put both your hands on your lower body, where your Sacral Chakra (and for women the womb) is located. Focusing on this part of the body, bring your attention to the wounds of sexual violence in your life. Allow tears to flow, angry screams to get out, stories to play in your head and maybe just silence to take over. When it's too much, slowly sit up and give yourself a moment to just be. When you are ready, grab a pen and paper and write down everything that is here. If it feels right, you can burn the paper after, or rip it apart and flush it through the toilet. If you want to keep it and re-read it, that is more than okay as well.

This exercise helped you check-in with your body and it's stories about sexual violence. Take a day, and reflect on what you feel needs attention first: do you want to work on your mind, your body, your energy field? Do you seek connection and a listening ear, or would you prefer to walk through the dark by yourself first?

—

The first step towards feeling better, is knowing how you are doing in the current moment. It's understanding what is alive in the body, and what are the stories you tell yourself. This takes honesty. I know it's oftentimes easier to diminish how we are feeling by telling ourselves all the positives in life. By looking towards the bright side, we hope that the negatives dissapear. From personal experience, I can tell you that this is not the case. Our pain will keep popping up until we are ready to face it, and that's totally okay. The more transparant we are with ourselves, even if it might sound ugly, the easier it get's to actually make a difference in our life.

If you feel like now is not the time to focus on it, take the time to stay busy with other things. It's okay to walk away from the pain for a while. It's okay to lose yourself in 'bad behavior'. Ofcourse, this is not a permissionslip to hurt those around you. To negatively impact the people around us by not taking responsibility for ourselves. However, I do feel like empathy and acceptance towards acting out due to trauma is fair. We should never enable it, but accepting it until someone is ready to face their pain is okay. It might sound controversial for a book about healing, yet I truly believe we all have our own path. Nobody can force us into being happy, feeling at ease, no matter how hard they try. Nobody can take our pain away, even if it's their biggest dream. Nobody knows better than the voice in our heart what we need, but it takes a lot of courage to start listening to it. And if you need time to build that courage, take it. As long as you are honest with yourself. This might look like this: 'I know that partying tonight will not bring me the calmth I am craving, but I do not have the power to face the pain in a way that will'. Awareness and acceptance of where you are, will lead to taking action to new ways of behavior once you are ready for it.

You are not a problem to be fixed. You are not a broken person, doomed for bad things. You are a beautiful person, who survived something terrible. You are a human, trying to live your life. You are not the love you receive, nor the opinions other's have about you. You are the love you give to others, even while you are hurting yourself. You are the efforts you put in showing up as a good person, even if nobody else sees them. You are not your trauma, you are simply a human who has experienced this. Even if it feels like the pain takes over everything, you have so many more characteristics. The way you smile at a stranger? Love to read a book when it rains? Any of the characteristics and behaviors that make you, you? That's who you are, not just the shame or the pain.

There is a fine line between self-pity, getting stuck in a cycle of comfortable pain or taking the time to get ready to face ourselves. The only person who can define this, is you. If someone points out your negative cycle, try to be open to their perspective without taking it personally. Respond to those who try to help you, but don't force yourself. Forcing ourselves into healing, can turn into hurting ourselves even more. It can hurt us even more, especially if it is rooted into the belief that we are not good enough. True healing comes from finding back our feeling of worthiness, the believe that we deserve to live a happy life. It is rooted in love.

Experiencing sexual violence was not our choice, or responsibility. Working our way back to a place of internal balance is. And guess what? It's not 'What doesn't kill you makes you stronger'. Trauma does not make you stronger, it breaks you down, brings you to your knees, makes you behave in self-destructive ways, makes you distrust life, maybe even hate yourself. What makes you stronger, is the little spark of hope in your heart that makes you take a baby step towards feeling better everyday. It's allowing the loving arms of your friends to hug you, listening to the supportive words of a professional and trusting it. It's choosing to do what is right for you, every day. Some days that little sparkle of hope may be prominent, and some days it might be far away from you.

Healing unfortunately does not mean going back to who you were before your experience. It means accepting all the broken pieces, that might even be on fire around you, and deciding that this is not the end. That you'll believe in yourself enough to start accepting help to build a new version of you that feels good. A version of you that will make all your dreams come true just for yourself. Ofcourse, our loved ones can be a motivation. Wanting to show up in a different way for those we love is beautiful. In the end, we do need to do it for us. A big part of healing is taking the leap and keep moving towards a different life, even is we have no clue how.

And this path? It will be rough. It will hurt even more than what you've experienced. It will be lonely. It will show you everything you love and hate about yourself. But a little glimpse of what's to come after: it's worth it, because you are worth it. You deserve to know and love yourself. You deserve to be the happiest you've ever been. Even if it will mean taking one step forward, taking ten steps back. Even if it means doing five sidequests. Stopping when it's to hard and then starting over ten times. This will be your journey, and you don't owe anyone an explanation. Ofcourse you owe everyone to treat them with respect, from a place of love. But you are allowed to walk this path in your way.

So thank you, thank you for taking these first steps together on a path towards being more balanced. I trust that you'll know exactly what you need to do, and hope that somewhere along the way you will trust this too. Know that the steps written down in this book are suggestions. If you have other ideas first, try those. If you want to do it in a different order, go for it. Allow yourself to have fun along the way as well. Allow yourself to follow your joy, even if you have no clue what this means. You'll get there. Mark your calander a year from now, and reflect by then how far you've come: it will surprise you!

The big question is: are you ready to work on yourself? Are you willing to make yourself a priority? Are you able to face the hurt you've experienced? Are you ready to lose your current identity and create a new life for yourself?

This might sound huge and scary, or too big of an commitment. It can even make you give up. So for now, I want to ask you whether you are willing to take a babystep everyday. Whether you are ready to give your best everyday. This might look like 10% one day, and 100% the next, as long as it is the best of your ability that day. Some days, that will be working to change your mindset, other days that will be taking a long nap and allowing yourself to rest.

Grab a pen and paper, and work write yourself a promiseletter. Promise yourself to do your best, while acknowledging it will look different each day. Write down why you think you are worth making this commitment, if you don't feel like you are, write why you are willing to try it anyway.

Make an honest appreciation of your current situation. Do you have physical problems that you have been ignoring for a longer amount of time? Make an appointment at your doctor and get it checked. Are you under treatment for something with a specialist? Check in with yourself whether you are giving these problems a 100% of your dedication. Do you get enough sleep and the right nutriments everyday? Do you take enough time and space for yourself to relax and clear your mind? Do you move your body a little bit on a daily basis? It's impossible to improve your current state of being, if your basic needs are not met. Make sure to ask for the support you need to meet them. It's okay to receive support, even if it feels awkward.

How is your mental health situation? If you are currently living with (C-)PTSD symptoms, it is important to find professional help. Some examples of these symptoms are: re-experiencing, anxiety, emotional dysregulation, dissociation, nightmares or insomnia, cynism about life and humanity. Also if you are strugling with panic attacks or anxiety in general. It is important to seek professional help. Specific trauma therapy like EMDR can help reduce some of your symptoms over time. It is brave and strong to seek mental help. Especially when we are talking about big topics like sexual violence, getting support of a trained professional, who you feel connected to, is very important.

Have you been strugling with substance abuse? Make agreements with yourself on when and how you'll use it from now on. Please don't struggle alone with this, if you have no clue where to start, find support by an anonymous group in your area or online. Have you been fighting suicidal thoughts, or any form of self-harm recently? You are not alone, this is nothing to be ashamed of. Please seek support of a trusted professional. This is not failing, this is the first and biggest win in this battle for survival.

For any professional you confide in, make sure it feels right. Mental help only works if there is a relationship of trust. It is important to know that the professional has been trained to support you in your process. But more than this, it is of upmost important you feel at ease around this person. It is no shame to ask for someone else if you don't feel any connection. Your doctor can help you find support, there are also many resources online where you can ask for free support or guidance towards a professional.

If you face a waitinglist or extended period of time in between your appointments, make sure you have the needed support during this waiting. Talk with someone you trust in your direct environment, find ways to reduce the intensity of this timeperiod or seek a holistic practicioner who helps you in different ways. Things as trauma-informed yoga can be found for free on YouTube, journalprompts, guided meditation, or energy healings can help you calm down in this moment.

Deciding to seek help might shake up your whole world, and in this totally normal. You might feel like the whole world trembles. It can feel empowering, or like you are just completely collapsing. This is all okay, try to give yourself the space to let it happen. Make sure to have the time and space to cry, dance, sing, scream, be overwhelmed. Maybe you'll naturally focus on something else and lose yourself in this, that's okay too. This first step is often times the hardest, and everyone responds to this in a different way.

Taking actual steps can make your pain feel real. This sounds silly, but as long as we keep it inside we can hide it. By taking the step to seek support, we bring it into the outerworld and we have to face it. This can lead to you minimizing the problem, feeling shame and guilt, maybe even thinking you're faking it all. Just observe it, discuss it with the professional you are reaching out to. These things are normal, sometimes our brain plays games with us. That does not mean that you are crazy, that you are doing the wrong thing. It can also lead to completely overtaking you, resulting in trying to numb the pain through many ways. Seek support to prevent self-harm.

Your Journey to Consent

Are you getting overstimulated? There are some simple tricks that can help! Grab some icecubes and allow them to melt into your hands making you feel the cold and water drip to change your current perspective. Another simple practice is to take 3 breaths, continued by out loud naming 5 things you can see, 4 things you touch, 3 things you hear, 2 things you smell and lastly 1 thing you taste. Go for a walk without music, just observing your surroundings and allowing your brain to slowly, but surely, stop racing. Plan in some time for yourself in your calender and do absolutely nothing, lay in bed eating snacks if you like, call a friend and share whatever is on your heart -after asking whether they have the space to listen.

—

To heal means to refind balance: you will need to rebuild a relationship with yourself. It is a journey to slowly feel at home in your own body again, to remember the voice of your heart and trust yourself. This is something that will happen gradually, over time. It is not a one-time decision, it is something that takes time.

In my opinion, refinding this balance is getting to know yourself on deeper levels and letting go of old identities consistently. It means taking the time to let go of the things that no longer serve you, and setting new intentions to pour love into yourself alternately. I will give you examples of both in the next paragraphs. Refinding your balance means working with a specific healing modality that speaks to you, but feeling free to try out new ones when you feel that your progress is getting stagnant.

In this process, it is good to find guidance and support. You can work together with a certain facilitator for a specific timeframe. As long as you always keep in mind that in the end, you are the one who is doing the work and everyone else can only hand you new tools. In my work, I tell my clients that I can help them reach a specific goal, but they will have to move forward without me afterwards. Ofcourse they can always call me for help if needed, but my goal is to make them realize that they have all they need inside of themselves. A good support is with you for a season in your life, but will not make you depend on them.

It is very important to find a facilitator you trust, who is able to hold the trauma-informed space for you and has the tools to guide you afterwards. Please always remember that consent is key. Nobody should tell you they have all the answers, or give you unasked advice. Nobody should randomly do energywork for you, without asking first. Support should always empower you, not leave you lost, scared or dependent. It is okay to listen to your gut in this, and walk away if something doesn't feel right. It is okay to ask someone what courses and studies they have done, as long as you realize that having certifications doesn't mean actually living the medicine. It is important to look at the standards a facilitator upholds, to see which values they embody and question whether this aligns with you.

Sometimes we want to embark on this journey without any support. There are amazing resources as books, documentaries, YouTube video's with information and even social media is full of practices. Know that, as long as you make sure you are safe, this is just as valuable as learning from someone else.

Before deciding which method of reconnecting with yourself you want to do, it is good to feel what you need. Take a moment to listen to your body by counting your breaths and sitting calmly. Grab a pen and paper and for 5 minutes answer the following prompt: 'what do I need right in this moment?'. Based on this answer, choose something you are already familiar with or something new!

There is no such thing as 'releasing' trauma. We can't just throw it away, and act as if it never happened. Nobody can support you to 'completely reset' in one session. Yes, a breathwork session can support you beautifully on your path. Yes, an Energy Healing can remove stagnant energy from your field. Yes, psychedelics can help you gain new perspectives. Yes, rituals can help you step onto a new path. But there is no such thing as a 'fasttrack' to healing, especially with sexual violence that rewired your nervous system, brain and heart. We need to integrate the lessons of those sessions in our daily life. We have to keep up the work to actually feel different when we wake up each day.

It is important to realize that real change comes from whitin and takes time. It takes dedication, little and big steps, a deep change of your whole system. We can't take a 'magic pill' that changes everything. It might be a lifetime of unlearning and rewiring your system. This path can be seen as a spiral: everytime we make the same circle we will meet the same pain, but on a deeper layer, in a new perspective.

There are many beautiful modalities that can help you let go of tension. Breathwork is a very popular and strong one, this can bring you back into the body, show you what is alive and help you move through it until it leaves the system. It can be extremely powerful to do a 1:1 session or take part in a group session. There are many plantmedicines which can help with this as well, for this it is extremely important to find a way to do this safely.

For women, a wombcleansing can help release energies that are not theirs. Or for everyone a guided meditation including 'cord-cutting' or 'calling your energy back' might make a huge difference. Doing an energy healing, like Reiki, and asking the facilitator to support you releasing all that is not yours. Another way is Myofascia massage, to release the tension of your body, or abdominal massage.

Does this all sound way too 'spiritual' for you? Going to a rageroom with the intention of just letting go of anger. Doing a boxingclass and letting yourself fully go in this moment. Going -sober!- for a dance and letting every feeling out. Shaking your body with your favorite music in the background. Writing all the things you want to forget on a plate and breaking it. Asking a friend to listen and just blurting it all out. Screaming into your pillow, or singing screaming while driving in your car. Going for a run outside. Diving into the ocean and asking it to wash all your worries away. These things can help you let go of some of the things you want to let go off, that might feel less strange to do!

It's time to let go a little bit of your rage, tension, doubt, fear, and any negative feeling! I will write out a practice you can do for yourself. While doing this, I want to invite you to listen to some music you thoroughly enjoy & which will help you to let go. Make sure to have a room for yourself where you can make noise and move as wanted, and nobody will interrupt you for a bit!

Start the moment in Balasana (Childspose) to really sink into the moment. Take as long as you need here, focussing on the breath and slowly arrive into the space. When you feel ready: set an intention for yourself. What do you want to let go off? What feelings are present? Why do you want to do this practice?

After this, it is time to shake! Make sure to have some nice music on and time at least 10 minutes. During those 10 minutes: there is no stopping! Start making slow movements, and keep shaking. You can shake your limbs, jump up and down, just move your hips. You can breath in slowly and release with as much sound as you want. Maybe you even want to incorporate some screaming, it's all okay! Do what feels natural to you.

After those 10 minutes, we will do a short Kundalini Kriya practice called Kashtha Takshanasana (Chopping wood). If you are a visual person, you can google the name and find many different examples. The idea is that you bring the hands together, when you breath in bring the hands all the way up: above the head; when you breath out, you bring the hands down and make a loud 'HA' sound. First, you sit in a Vajrasana (Thunderbolt) position, which is a seated on the knees (kneeling position) with a straight spine. Afterwards you will do the Malasana (Yogic squat) where you sit in a deep squat with the knees pointed outwards and the spine straight. Lastly, you stand up straight, feet shoulderwith and when you bring the arms down you do an additional squat. You will do three sets in each position, each time until failure and with 30 seconds of rest in between. After this series, you lay down in Savasana (corpse pose) which is straight on the back, fully relaxed with extended arms and legs for 5-10 minutes.

Slowly find your way to a seated position and grab a pen and paper. Take ten minutes to write everything down you are ready to let go. This can be a letter to someone else, a list of negative believes, all the frustrations you feel or simply what comes up in the moment. Afterwards, if it feels right you can read it one last time. When you are ready to let go, you burn the papers (in a safe way!).

Make sure to stay in silence for at least 30 minutes after doing this practice. Spend as much time with yourself as needed and drink enough water! You might want to go for a walk, take a long shower, chat with a friend or eat some nourishing food. It might sound easy, but a practice like this can have a strong influence on how you are feeling or work in your energyfield for some time.

Refinding balance does not mean leaving parts of you, or only feeling better. Sometimes it means transmuting negative things into something beautiful. Other times it means setting a new intention. Or it can mean giving yourself the love you always deserved. It might even be just telling yourself how beautiful you are or reflecting on how far you've come and being incredibly proud of yourself. It means slowly seeing your worth, which is something that is always there instead of tied to what you do for others.

Healing from sexual violence means slowly falling in love with who you are again. Allowing the 'ugly' and 'beautiful' parts of you to co-exist, and finding beauty in it. Re-discovering joy in being alive, allowing yourself to laugh in places where you once cried. It means claiming back your body, and slowly feeling okay with touch. These steps are often less loud than releasing, it might go by silently and you realize it after months.

However, it is not as easy as this sounds. The first time you feel at home in your body again, you might be confronted with all the negative things that live here as well. When you trust someone with your story, you might feel incredibly vulnerable and scared after. When you feel pride in who you are, you might feel a rush of sadness for who you had to be. Entering a new intimate relationship, might bring up new realizations of how you've always deserved more than what you experienced. And all these 'negative' emotions when you have a win? They are completely okay. They are natural, it simply means you feel safe enough to face the hurt.

Go easy on yourself, please. It's not a race to feel okay all of the time. Over time, you will be the happiest you've ever been. However, we can only feel as much happiness as the sadness we allow ourselves to feel. There is no short-cut to a long, happy after. This is to be found in the small things, only to realize that those small things have taken over your daily life.

There are many ways to center you in the moment, make you feel really good and relaxed. Doing a cacaoceremony can help you to reconnect to your heart, feel your emotions and just be present in the moment. A long walk in nature, a danceparty in your home or a loving conversation with someone you trust can bring the same. A sound-healing is a beautiful way to relax and bring yourself to a specific frequency, where you might feel more loving towards yourself or which can bring you a new perspective.

Practices like Yoga Nidra and meditation can help you softly rewire your brain, bring relaxation into your system or just feel loving energy. EFT tapping can help you to rewire your whole system. A long bath, energetic massage, Chakra balancing or energy healing like Reiki or craniosacral therapy can create a safe space for you to relax and simply be. Doing an art project, cooking a nice meal or baking something can be a good method as well.

Doing bodywork helps slowly taking back control. Consent based contact improv (a form of dancing) can feel extremely vulnerable, but teach you that touch is safe and beautiful. Learning self-defence can be empowering and make you feel safer in yourself. As long as you remember that not having been able to fight is not something to be ashamed of.

Doing things you loved as a child: climbing a tree, running around on the beach, diving into a river, can make you feel free and reconnected with the body as well. Having a weighted blanket can help you find calmth, or hugging someone you love.

Oracle readings can help you gain new perspective on a certain situation. If you have questions surrounding a specific topic, this can help you think outside the box, or it might confirm what you were feeling before. Shadow-work and specific journalprompts can help you to find our strengths in the chaos of your pain. Working through limiting believes or using affirmations can also help you put new ideas in your head.

Joining a Kirtan or singing circle with medicine songs opens up your heart to joy. An estatic dance also helps to bring joy into your system and transmute any frustration into joy. Creating a visionboard, journaling about your dreams and thinking of ways to get there is also a strong way to bring in new energy into your life.

Diving into the world of consent, for example with the consent wheel, can help you to understand more and more what your boundaries and pleasure are. Diving into Tantra, can help you reconnect with the fact that your body is a temple. It is all about being aware in the moment and your body. It is important to note that Tantra is not equal to sex, and it is extremely important to always protect your boundaries in practices like this. There are a lot of solo practices you can do!

It's time to bring in some new energy into your life! Take a moment first with yourself to set the setting: do you want to make a beautiful altar with some things to celebrate yourself or life? Do you want to make yourself a nice cup of tea? Make sure to create a safe setting where you are free to express yourself and won't get interrupted for the next hours.

Start by setting up your favorite song, a nice suggestion: if you ever forget - Anouk & Yora, and do a little dance with yourself, or simply listen to the song with your eyes closed. When you feel present in the moment, focus on your breathing and slowly connect with your body. When you are here, set an intention for this beautiful moment with yourself.

Start by writing down three things you are grateful for, but make them about you! Think about what you find good characteristics of yourself, achievements you are proud off, or lessons you have learned. Once you have done this, take 10 minutes to write down 1 dream for yourself, if it feels better you can also make an artwork which represents it, or a visionboard.

Grab a paper and write down a list of things that are holding you back to achieve this. Are there things that feel unease around this dream? Stories you tell yourself that make it impossible? When you are done, cross them with a different pen, and write positive affirmations down that counter the limiting beliefs.

It's time to move! With the feeling of achieving the dream, go for a long walk while visualizing it to happen. Listen to some positive frequencies and dance around to the idea of already living your dream. Do some nice relaxing yoga, or some self-care that help you sink into the body even more.

Lastly, take 30 minutes for yourself in silence. Sit with yourself in this renewed energy. Let yourself feel the joy, allow it to become normal in your nervous system. Complete this session by looking at yourself in the mirror and telling yourself the new possitive affirmations.

Healing is done in community. To start your journey, it might feel very safe to keep it all for yourself: this is more than okay! However, you can only do so much yourself or in 1:1 sessions. We as humans are made to connect, we are 'group animals' so to say. Our nervous system regulates in connection to others. We can learn to feel safe in the presence of other people. Doing work in groups can show you the things you overlook or are unable to see yourself. It can give you new perspectives and sometimes hearing and seeing other's perspectives makes that we do not have to learn that lesson ourselves.

Shame and the feeling of isolation, loss of your voice plays a big role in the pain of survivors of sexual violence. Therefore, it is incredibly powerful to be witnessed by others in your process of healing. Speaking up in a safe environment can help you reclaim your voice and autonomy. Feeling that others are standing besides you, and support you in your journey helps you to step back into your power.

Learning to allow intimacy back in, in 1:1 relationships or safe containers can help to return fully back in the body. A lot of survivors have trouble with intimacy, get triggered by physical touch, don't trust those around you anymore. This is a wound that only gets healed in relation to others. Having a person, or being guided by someone back into conscious physical touch, sharing meals and laughter can make it easier.

Sharing rage and anger can help in the feeling of community, and realization that no matter how terrible your experience: it is not your mistake and you are not alone in this pain. Shared grieve is easier to carry than having to do it all by yourself. It can be easier to speak up, advocate, learn together.

It is important to find people you truly feel safe and good with. Don't rush into connection, it is okay to take the time to find out whether you feel like someone is safe to explore this with. The right people will never make you feel like you are 'too much' 'too needy' or 'crazy'. The right container for you will feel genuine, like all of you is welcome here and it will make you feel safe to be uncomfortable. Opening up again will be scary, you will be mirrored back things you don't want to see, you might be held accountable, but this is all part of the medicine.

An amazing form of community is a men's or women's circle. These are containers where people from the same gender come together to be witnessed in who they are. Sometimes you might have a sharingcircle, sometimes you will do practices, sometimes you will learn information on specific topics. You can find those places in-person or online. I have an bi-weekly, online, donation-based womxn's circle for everyone who identifies as a woman and contacts for a men's circle: feel free to reach out!

In close friendships, a loving family relationship or intimate relationship there is a deep opportunity to heal and share as well. It is good to practice this slowly. Choose someone who is close to you, and first ask them whether they are open to have a conversation on the topic of sexual violence. Everyone has different triggers and experiences, therefore it is important to make sure someone is comfortable before starting to share.

You can start by simply sharing that you are currently working to refind balance after having an (in)direct experience with sexual violence. Another option is to share one thing you've learned from this book and ask what their opinion is on this.

Keep in mind that even if it is scary, opening a conversation like this always helps both parties! By asking someone to have this conversation with you, you make it easier for them next time to ask you for a conversation like this. It is important to realize that you have to feel safe in a conversation like this. Make sure to have an environment where you can share openly, and feel okay to let emotions move through you. Agree on a 'safeword' which you can use to stop the conversation without an explanation if you get triggered. Listen to hear, do not give any unasked advice. If you want to share your perception to the other person, ask them whether this is okay first. And keep it as light as you want, if you after five minutes want to joke about something: that's okay! Make sure to create a judgement free situation, where you allow each to just freely share without being afraid.

Thank each other after the conversation, and make sure to check-in later that day or the day after to see whether both are still feeling okay.

—

Where doing the above mentioned practices and workshops can be good, your daily habits make the biggest impact on your life! Setting an intention each day to reconnect with yourself and do the best you can is a very good start. Making sure that your basic needs: a feeling of safety, enough rest, nourishing food, a feeling of community, and autonomy over your process are met. Somedays, this will be all that you get to do for yourself, and that is completely okay. As long as you keep in mind, that most things in life are a matter of priority: we all have the same 24-hours in a day, it is up to you to decide how you fill those. Yes ofcourse we have work, social obligations and personal circumstances: but making healing a priority is always your own choice. Doing something small for yourself can exist of 5 minutes when you wake up to name 3 things you are thankful for: you don't need an elaborate practice of three hours each day!

Once you have fulfilled your basic needs, I love to ask the people I work with to do something for each of the five Koshas. The five Koshas come from the Vedic tradition and include: Annamaya Kosha (the physical body); Pranamaya Kosha (the energetic body); Manomaya Kosha (the mental and emotional body); Vijnamaya Kosha (the wisdom body) and the Anandamaya Kosha (The Bliss body).

For the Annamaya Kosha (the physical body), we have to think about how to take care of our physique. On some days this might consist of a long walk, other days a work-out and in other moments it might be going to the Sauna or getting a massage. It's all about moving, nourishing, and listening to the body. Deciding what to do for this can be intuitively, as long as one really listens to the body instead of forcing something specific.

To work on the Pranamaya Kosha (the energetic body), is a little more spiritual. This is our subtle body, one we cannot grasp, but where our life-force energy moves. A very useful, and less 'woo-woo' tactic for this is to do some pranayama, or breathwork. You can do a Nadi Shodhana, which is alternative nostril breathing, to balance this body. But also doing some Kundalini-yoga; some energywork for oneself or receiving Reiki can be part of this step.

To tend to the Manomaya Kosha (the mental and emotional body) means taking the time to understand the monkey-mind and allowing your emotions to stream freely through yourself. A very useful tactic can be to journal daily: doing some morningpages to write down whatever is going on in your brain. Another idea is to go to therapy or practice mindfulness by doing some art.

Practices for the Vijnamaya Kosha (the wisdom body) is to connect with your intuition, the soft voice of your heart. This is all about inner-knowing. To listen to this, you need inner silence: it can be good to do a meditation, just spend time in absolute silence or pull some oracle cards to reconnect with the voice whitin.

Reconnecting with the Anandamaya Kosha (The Bliss body) is all about feeling the love and joy of the universe inside of you. This is about devotion to yourself, to god, to love, the universe. You can do this through Bhakti Yoga (chanting Mantra's), through just dancing in your room or do something that fills you with you. Another easy practice is to write down three things you are grateful for.

Are you ready to embark on your journey? Start small! Let's make a little calender, online or on paper, where you can tick off having done your practices for the next 21 days. You can start small by doing 1 thing a day, or do all 5 above described practices. Make a special bubble for every 7th day, to celebrate your progress!

After the 21 days, reflect on your progress. Keep in mind, doing something for yourself for 21 days straight is already a huge accomplishment. You don't need to change your life drastically and immediatly. Taking babysteps into the right direction is still progress. Did you miss a day? Well, you are human! It is still good to celebrate having the intention to do so, keep up the amazing work.

***

May this journey to consent be a starting point for you, those around you and society. There are lots of things to be discovered along the way. And probably if you redo the exercises, there are new discoveries inside of you.

You can go way deeper into the topic of pleasure and consent if that's what you desire. But you can also stay here and just live with your full-body yes and no. Do whatever lights you up, as long as you listen to yourself.

The biggest form of rebellion in the current state of the world: someone who enjoys safe, consensual sex in their own way without any performance or co-ercion. So please go experience the world as fun, sex in itself is one of the most beautiful ways of connection between two people, it can be filled with pleasure and create magic in your life. Because we all deserve a world filled with love, and we will create it one by one.

But remember, you cannot be free, if other's are not free. Once you feel good in your own body, and balanced: please help to bring this balance into the world. Listen to those who share about their pain, support those who are fighting to reconnect with themselves in your own way, speak up when you see something that isn't aligned with your values. Every little action helps us rebuild a world in which we are free of this terrible problem.

If this book helped you to find your balance, give it forward to someone else who might need this balance as well. You are always welcome to share your journey with me, or see whether there is an opportunity to walk this path together.

Thank you.

—

Nadine Donselaar

Desire

A power feared by many, strength in it's rawest form.

Pure love, pure freedom.

A lightning, with the ability to destroy or create.

Sexual energy, primal force

The most beautiful, yet painful thing I know

It ruined me, yet it brought me sso much joy

Relentless, yet innocent

Tears during an orgasm,

Replacing scars with gardens of love

Sex, It's a game for the fearless and trustworthy

Are you ready to surrender to connection

To take turns to lead, turns to follow

Moments or intensity, times of calmth

A flirty relationship build on trust.

A safe body opens up to depths one can only dream off,

Sex turns into a sacred language.

About the Author

As a young woman, Nadine Donselaar combines her passion for Social Justice and Holistic Health in a dream to make this world more beautiful. With a double Master degree in Law - focused on Human Right Rights- and working in the Holistic Health sector offering several practices as Reiki, Kundalini Yoga, Oracle Readings, Guidance she has a unique perspective on the world. This perspective gets fueled by her frequent travels around the world, allowing her to experience different cultures.

You can find my online services here:

www.nadinedonselaar.com

(http://www.nadinedonselaar.com)

You can read more from me on my substack:

@nadinedonselaar

You can find free meditations and practices on youtube:

Nadine Donselaar

Or follow me on Instagram and tiktok

@nadine.donselaar

www.ingramcontent.com/pod-product-compliance
Lightning Source LLC
Chambersburg PA
CBHW042128160426
43198CB00021B/2942